SMALL

QUILTCRAFTS

S · M · A · L · L
QUILTCRAFTS
BY JENNIFER GEIGER

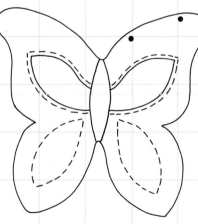

SEDGEWOOD® PRESS
NEW YORK, N.Y.

ACKNOWLEDGEMENTS

This book was put together under the gracious and intelligent direction of some very creative people. It gives me great pleasure to thank:

Dina von Zweck, for her outstanding perception and guiding spirit.

Betty Rice, for her professional expertise and superb patience.

Lane Berkwit, for the photos that were so carefully planned and taken.

Larry Bilotti, at Laura Ashley, for helping in the selection of fabrics used as background in many of the photos.

Laura Ashley fabrics used as background in photos on pages 46, 53, 60, 79, 87, 130, 140.

Laura Ashley lace panel used in photos on pages 38, 42, 107, 120.

Laura Ashley tiles used in photo on page 87.

Editorial Director: *Dina von Zweck*

For Sedgewood® Press
Director: *Elizabeth P. Rice*
Project Manager: *Connie Schrader*
Project Editor: *Carol Anderson*
Production Manager: *Bill Rose*
Design: *Bentwood Studio/Jos. Trautwein*
Photography: *Lane Berkwit*

Distributed by Meredith Corporation, Des Moines, Iowa.
ISBN: 0-696-02319-9
Library of Congress Catalog Card Number: 88-061382

Printed in the United States of America

10 9 8 7 6 5 4 3 2 1

TO

my mother,

MARTHA GILL

CONTENTS

HOME AND HEARTH

REST EASY

COZY KITCHEN

INTRODUCTION

Creating and preparing SMALL QUILTCRAFTS has given me enormous pleasure. In this book you will find exciting projects and easy-to-follow instructions. Whether you are a beginner or an experienced needleworker, this book will be a treasure trove to be used over and over again.

Many of the patterns and colors in the book are derived from my rural Pennsylvania heritage. At an early age I was exposed to the rich variety of bold colors and geometric patterns that are so prevalent in the Pennsylvania Dutch, Mennonite, and Amish traditions. My real interest in quilting began at a country auction when I bought a bag filled with muslin squares, each of which had been embroidered in red to form the outline of an animal. I stitched them together, then quilted them using a quick-and-easy technique called tied quilting. The result was a small quilt for my son, Ian. He loved it, and he soon learned to identify and name the various animals.

Throughout America, I discovered, there has been a great, renewed interest in quilting — sparked in part by magazines, museum shows, country fairs, and contests.

The sophisticated, eye-catching designs being created by women all over the country are an amazing sight. These quilters are turning scraps of fabric (often salvaged from old cloths) into works of art, and so can you. You can also create small, practical items for yourself as well as for family and friends.

My inspiration for this book comes from those small, portable projects that can be "carried along" and are relatively quick to make. The book is designed to introduce and share with you an outstanding variety of ideas and projects that are rewarding to make, fun to use, and a pleasure to give as gifts. Everything from Grandmother's Fan Tablecloth, Country Biscuits Pillow, and Babushka Tea Cozy to Cupid's Quiver Sachet Pocket, Baby's-Block Nap Pad, and Quilted Critters — is here for your satisfaction and enjoyment.

These projects also offer a rich variety of easy-to-stitch quilting techniques: hand quilting, machine quilting, crazy quilting, log-cabin quilting, tied quilting, and ribbon quilting. So plan on showing off your talent by making these stunning designs both for yourself and as special gifts.

GENERAL DIRECTIONS

BEFORE YOU START

Before beginning any of the projects in this book, be sure to read all of the General Directions to familiarize yourself with the basic techniques used. In some cases the directions for individual projects refer to the General Directions for more detailed instruction.

QUILTING TERMS

Special terms are used to describe the quilting processes. These terms are used in the quilting directions in this book. Also, different kinds of quilts each have their own names. This list will help you understand how quilts are made, and make the quilting directions easy to follow.

Backing
Bottom layer of quilted piece. This can be made from lightweight cotton fabric or muslin.

Bias
Forty-five degree angle between the warp and the weft, where fabric has the most stretch.

Bias Strips
Strips of fabric cut on the bias and used to finish the edges of quilted items.

Biscuit Quilting
Puffed quilt made by machine-stitching small stuffed fabric squares or "biscuits" together.

Calico
Cotton fabric with small floral pattern that contrasts background.

Contour Quilting
Lines of quilting outside the contours of appliqués or patchwork pieces.

Counterpane
The design is quilted over an entire area with no embellishment of patchwork or appliqué.

Crazy Quilt
Assorted, irregularly shaped fabric scraps or patches are pinned or basted, with the edges overlapping, to the muslin backing. Raw edges are turned under and patches are slip-stitched to muslin. All edges of patches may be covered with fancy hand-embroidery stitches.

Log Cabin
A contrasting center block surrounded by strips or "logs" to create a specific design.

Patchwork
Sewing together small fabric shapes to form a larger geometric design.

Ribbon or Strip Quilting
Narrow strips of fabric or ribbons are stitched side by side directly onto batting and backing fabric or stitched to paper that is then removed.

Self-Finished Edges
Leaving a narrow band of excess backing fabric that can be folded, then stitched to the quilt front to form a binding.

Selvage
Finished edges along the length of the fabric (best removed before stitching fabric to prevent puckering).

Seminole Piecing
Strips of fabric are sewn together by machine. These are then marked and cut into sections. The sections are pieced together and sewn to form various new designs.

Template
Guide for marking fabric (used in both cutting and quilting).

Trapunto
Stuffing the underside of a design or appliqué to achieve a padded, sculptured effect.

14

BASIC TOOLS AND EQUIPMENT

The following is a list of tools and equipment needed to produce the quilted items in this book.

Batting

This is a soft filler used to stuff between layers of quilted fabric. Battings are sold by the yard or prepackaged sheets in standard quilt sizes. For the projects in this book, 100 percent bonded polyester batting was used.

Beeswax

This wax is used for coating sewing thread to reduce knotting or tangling.

Compass

You can use a plate, or any round form, but a compass is helpful for drawing circles.

Dressmaker's carbon paper

When marking fabric and transferring designs, this paper is useful.

Dressmaker's pins

Holding fabric in place while sewing makes for a neater finish.

Dressmaker's shears

The bent-handle shears with 7" or 8" blades make cutting fabric easier.

Embroidery floss

Six-strand floss is used for stitching embroidered projects and tied quilting. Use three of the six strands unless otherwise specified.

Embroidery hoop

Holding fabric while embroidering is made easier with a hoop.

Embroidery scissors

These small scissors with 3" or 4" blades are used for accurate trimming of threads and for cutting small pieces of fabric.

Felt tip pens

When enlarging and marking patterns, these pens are helpful.

Fusible interfacing

Used to strengthen and give body to lightweight fabrics, this material has one side that bonds to another fabric when pressed with a hot iron.

Graph or quadrille paper

Enlarging patterns is an easy job with these aids.

Knitting needle

Use a blunt-end needle for turning stitched objects right-side-out and for stuffing small, hard-to-reach areas.

Needles

Quilting betweens for quilting, sharps for handsewing, embroidery needles for embroidery.

Paper scissors

Cut paper patterns with these scissors.

Pencils, tailor's chalk, slivers of soap, and pastel pencils

Marking fabric can be done with any of these markers.

Polyester stuffing

Pillows, toys, and other items can be stuffed with polyester. Use one that is soft, fluffy and of even consistency.

Quilting hoops

Used to hold fabric while quilting; these are optional.

Quilting thread

For hand and machine quilting, the specially processed thread is made of waxed cotton or polyester-wrapped thread and is stronger than regular sewing thread.

Safety pins

When drawing elastic through a casing and turning fabric tubes, a selection of pins is helpful.

Seam ripper

Unwanted stitches are ripped quickly with this tool.

Sewing machine

All projects require sewing with this time-saver.

Sewing thread

Thread is used in many ways; select a dual duty, all-purpose thread for hand and machine sewing.

Steam iron and ironing board

Always press fabric before beginning a project.

Tape measure

Used for measuring three-dimensional objects and fabric, it is handy to carry with you.

Thimble

Used for quilting, hand-stitching, and embroidery to protect middle finger of hand that guides needle and underneath finger of opposite hand. Get used to using a thimble.

Tracing Paper

Used for transferring and enlarging patterns.

Twelve-inch see-through plastic ruler

Look for one with clearly marked numbers. It will be used for enlarging patterns, measuring fabric, and marking quilting lines.

BASIC TIPS
AND TECHNIQUES

ENLARGING PATTERNS

To enlarge the patterns in this book you will need a grid of 1" squares. To make a master grid that can be used repeatedly, use a pencil and ruler to mark a grid of 1" squares on a large sheet of paper (approximately 14" × 18"). Smaller sheets of paper can be taped together to form one large sheet.

Sheets of blue graph or quadrille paper can also be purchased at an art-supply store, and some sewing-supply stores sell a special 1" grid paper made for enlarging patterns.

To enlarge a pattern, tape a piece of tracing paper large enough to fit the final pattern onto the master grid. Using dots to mark where the pattern lines intersect, copy the reduced pattern onto the enlarged grid square by square. Connect the dots on the enlarged grid to get the final pattern drawing. Draw any other pattern markings onto the pattern. Cut out the pattern.

If you wish to enlarge only one pattern without making a master grid, draw a grid directly onto the tracing paper, then draw the pattern directly onto the grid.

To make a pattern larger or smaller, simply increase or reduce the size of the squares on the grid. For example, to make a pattern twice as large, just rule a grid of 2" squares.

TRANSFERRING PATTERNS AND PATTERN MARKINGS ONTO FABRIC

Before you begin to cut out patterns, press fabric and check grain line. Lay fabric out on a large flat surface. If the instructions indicate that fabric should be folded double, fold with selvage edges together. Before you begin cutting, place pattern pieces on fabric as close together as possible. Line up straight grain of fabric with the top and bottom of each pattern piece. Place patterns marked "place on fold" on the fold of the fabric. Pin patterns into place on the fabric. With a pencil, tailor's chalk or soap sliver, outline each pattern piece onto the fabric.

To transfer pattern markings onto fabric, decide which side of the fabric is to be marked. Most dots are marked on the wrong side, while quilting lines, pocket placement, and other pattern markings are marked on the right side of the fabric. Place dressmaker's carbon paper between the pattern and the fabric, or underneath the fabric, as specified. Trace markings directly onto the fabric.

Some pattern markings can be temporarily marked by placing a pin through the pattern and the fabric. Carefully lift the pattern, then replace the pin with a pencil marking. Many fabrics are thin enough to allow the pattern markings to be traced through the fabric. A sunny window or light box can also be used. Tape the pattern to the glass, then tape the fabric over it and trace over pattern markings.

CHOOSING FABRICS

Specific fabrics are listed for each project. When cotton is called for, use 100% cotton whenever possible to achieve professional-looking, long-lasting results. Other fabrics may be substituted for those listed, but for best results try to use a similar material. When in doubt, use your own judgment or consult a salesperson.

Different prints or colors may be substituted for most of the fabrics specified for each project. If you change the main fabric color, how-ever, be sure to coordinate all other fabrics and notions to match.

PRESSING FABRICS

Press all fabrics before beginning a project. Test-iron on a scrap of fabric to prevent scorching or crushing. Press all seams, hems, folds, and other fabric parts when indicated in the instructions. This saves time in the long run because sewing is made easier and more accurate. Pressing also gives a more professional look to the finished project. Remember, quilted items cannot be pressed without flattening the batting.

HAND QUILTING

Quilted pieces are made up of three layers: a decorative top piece with batting or filler in the center and a backing piece at the bottom. The layers are first basted together and then stitched permanently with small, evenly placed running stitches or tied with embroidery floss or yarn (tufting).

When the quilt top is finished, always cut the batting and backing larger than the top. Place the backing fabric right side down on a flat surface. Place batting on backing, smoothing out any wrinkles. Place the quilt-top piece right side up on the batting to create a "quilt sandwich."

To baste layers together, use a large needle and heavy thread. Begin at the center and work outward to the edges, keeping top and bottom layers smooth and even. Always baste on cross and lengthwise grains to prevent the fabric from stretching.

To quilt, use a short length of thread (about 18") and "lose the end" by pulling the knot through the bottom layer and embedding it in the batting. Stitching along marked lines, push the needle straight down through all layers with one hand. With the other hand, push the needle back up through the top, close to the point at which it was first inserted. With experience, you can make two to four stitches on the needle at once before pulling the needle all the way through; this is done by holding the fabric between the thumb and forefinger and keeping the needle at a slant. Always make sure the needle goes all the way through to the back of the quilt so that the stitching looks the same on both front and back.

Make the stitches as small as possible, approximately 10 to 12 stitches per inch. When you reach the end of the thread, make a few small backstitches and "lose the end."

"LOSING AN END"

To begin quilting, make a small knot at the end of the thread. Bring the needle up through the quilt to the top layer of the fabric. Gently pull the knot through the backing fabric, embedding it in the batting. Start quilt stitches.

When you run out of thread, backstitch a few times; then run the needle and thread through the top layer of the fabric and batting. Bring the needle up and out about an inch from the backstitching. Clip the thread close to the fabric. The thread end will sink back into the batting.

MACHINE QUILTING

Machine quilting is done with a straight stitch and allows the use of heavier fabrics and thicker batting. The layers must be firmly basted together to prevent them from shifting during quilting. Starting at the center and working outward, baste the layers together horizontally and vertically.

Set machine-stitch length at 8 to

12 stitches per inch. Release pressure on the presser foot slightly so that quilt layers can pass under it easily. Keep upper and lower tensions balanced so the stitches will be evenly locked on both sides. Guide the quilt under the presser foot by holding it with both hands, one in front and one behind the presser foot. Maintain an even, steady tension without pulling the fabric.

When quilting a large piece, try to keep the bulk of it to the left of the presser foot. Avoid pulling the part being stitched by placing a small table or several chairs to the left of the machine to support the bulk of the quilt. The piece may also be rolled from one end, then pinned to hold the roll in place while quilting.

TYING QUILTS

Thread the needle with embroidery floss, yarn, or strong thread. Starting on the top layer of the quilt, push the needle down through the fabric and backing, leaving a thread end of 2". Push the needle back up through the quilt a short distance away, leaving a small stitch on the backing fabric. Insert the needle back into

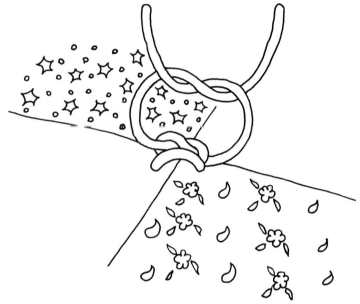

the top layer of the quilt, making a second stitch over the first. Tie the thread ends securely with a square knot, then trim evenly.

CLIPPING, NOTCHING, AND TRIMMING SEAM ALLOWANCE

To prevent curved stitched seams from puckering or pulling, clip inwardly curved seams almost to the seam allowance. Outwardly curved seams are notched by cutting out small wedges of fabric to eliminate bulkiness. Before turning stitched pieces right side out, trim seam allowance diagonally at corners to create less bulk and to achieve a sharper corner.

BINDING EDGES

Lining up the raw edges, place fabric strip or bias tape right sides together with the fabric. If the ends of the binding meet, fold one end under ¼″ so that it overlaps the opposite end. Stitch fabric to binding with ¼″ seam or as specified. Turn the binding over the seam allowance. Fold the edge of binding strip under so the fold is even with the stitching line. Slip-stitch the folded edge of the binding to the fabric.

STUFFING PROJECTS

The projects in this book are stuffed with polyester stuffing. Stuff small areas and hard-to-reach places first, using a knitting needle or chopstick to push bits of stuffing into place. Stuff larger areas using handfuls of stuffing and working your way out to the fabric opening. To avoid lumps and bumps, stuff projects firmly and evenly.

Save leftover pieces of quilt batting. These can also be used in place of polyester stuffing when stuffing small objects.

HAND APPLIQUÉ

Cut-out pieces of fabric are sewn to a larger background material. After cutting out the appliqué piece, the raw edges are turned under; straight edges can be pressed under, while curved edges can be basted or finger-creased with the thumbnail. Edges can also be turned under with the thumb and forefinger while stitching.

Appliqués are first pinned or basted into place on a background, then stitched with an invisible slip stitch, keeping appliqué fabric smooth and even. Do not press stitched appliqués since turned-under edges will show through to the front of the fabric.

In pieced appliqué, smaller fabric cut-outs are stitched together to form a larger appliqué piece. This is then basted and slip-stitched to a background fabric.

STITCHING THE PROJECTS

MACHINE STITCHING

The projects in this book were for the most part sewn with a sewing machine using a straight or zigzag stitch. A small amount of hand stitching and embroidery was also used. Set the sewing machine at 12 stitches per inch when straight stitching. To prevent skipped stitches, use the proper size needle for each fabric.

Machine Zigzag Stitching

This stitch is used to join fabric pieces together, to embroider, to machine-appliqué, or to finish an edge. For best results, follow the directions that come with your sewing machine.

Machine Topstitching

This stitch decoratively joins two pieces of fabric together. On the right side of the fabric, make a row of stitches the desired distance from the fabric edge or seam. Stitch through all layers of the fabric.

HAND STITCHES

Basting Stitch

This stitch is used to hold fabrics together temporarily before stitching permanently. Basting stitches are larger versions of running stitches, usually ½" to 1" in length. Do not knot thread ends, so that stitches may be removed easily.

Running Stitch

This stitch is used for quilting, gathering, or hand-sewing seams that are not subjected to much strain. Work the needle in and out of the fabric until you have several tiny, even stitches. Pull the needle and thread through the fabric and start the next series of stitches. Quilting stitches should be small and evenly placed.

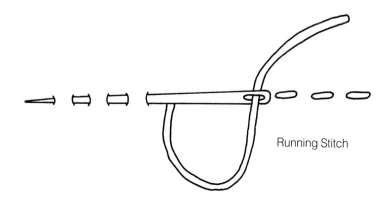

Running Stitch

Slip Stitch

This is an almost invisible stitch used to join two folded edges of a fabric, to hem, and to hold pockets and similar pieces in place. Slip the needle through the folded edge of the top fabric. Make a small stitch through the under fabric, then slip the needle back through the folded edge of the top fabric. When stitching two folded edges, slip the needle back and forth through the fabric folds. Space stitches evenly ⅛″ to ¼″ apart.

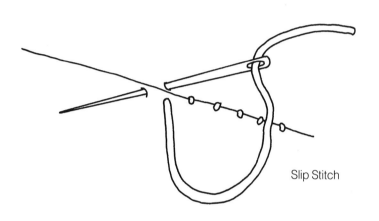

Slip Stitch

EMBROIDERY STITCHES

Embroidery is used to stitch the facial features and other details on various projects in this book. Use three strands of the 6-strand embroidery floss when stitching to allow for easier insertion of thread into the fabric and to achieve more accurate results.

Backstitch

This stitch is used for sewing embroidery outlines. Begin at the right end of the line to be covered or seam to be sewn. Bring the needle up through the fabric to the right side. Insert the needle back into the fabric ⅛″ behind the starting point. Bring the needle up ⅛″ in front of the starting point. Continue inserting the needle back to the last stitch and bringing it up one stitch ahead.

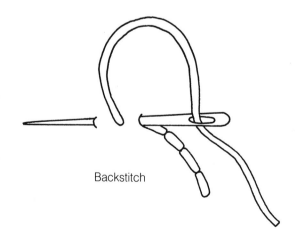

Backstitch

Blanket Stitch

This stitch is worked from left to right. Bring the needle through the fabric to the right side on the line to be covered. Insert the needle back into the fabric above the line a short distance to the right. Keeping the thread beneath the needle, bring the needle out directly below on the line and catch a loop of thread in a new stitch.

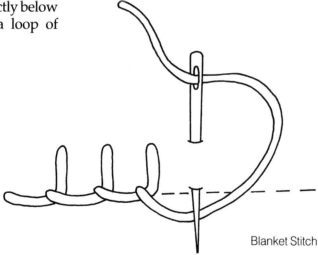

Blanket Stitch

Chain Stitch

This is a link stitch worked from right to left. Bring the needle up through the fabric at the right side of the line to be covered. Insert the needle back into the fabric beside the point where the thread emerged. Holding the thread to form a loop, bring the needle up a short distance to the left. Draw the thread through the loop. To make the second stitch, insert the needle inside the loop beside the point where the thread emerged and repeat the stitch.

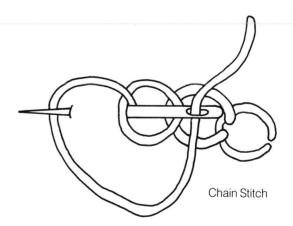

Chain Stitch

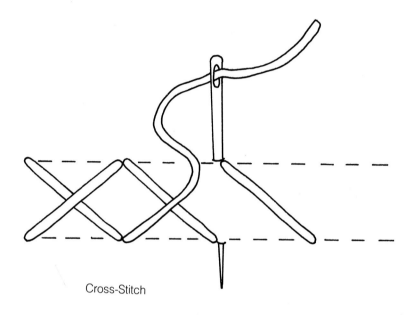

Cross-Stitch

Cross-Stitch

This stitch is made by stitching two separate rows of diagonal stitches. Starting at the lower right corner of the line to be covered, bring the needle through the fabric to the right side. Make a diagonal stitch to the upper left corner. Continue making evenly spaced diagonal stitches until the entire line is covered. Working from left to right, stitch a row of diagonal stitches across the first row, inserting the needle at the ends of the stitches.

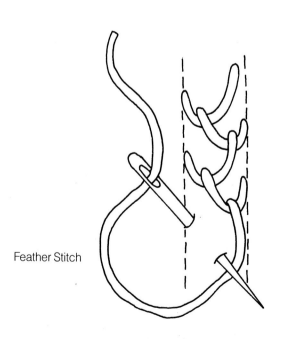

Feather Stitch

Feather Stitch

This stitch is worked from top to bottom. Bring the needle up to the right side of the fabric right of the area to be covered. Insert the needle back into the fabric below and to the left of the point where the thread emerged. Keeping the thread beneath the needle, bring the needle up near the center of the previous stitch; insert the needle below and slightly to the right of the area to be covered. With the thread beneath the needle, bring the needle up near the center of the previous stitch; insert the needle below and to the left of the area to be covered. Continue alternating stitches to the right and left until the area is filled.

Fly Stitch

This is a V-shaped stitch held in place by a vertical stitch that may vary in length. Beginning at the left end of the line to be covered, bring the needle up to the right side of the fabric above the line. Insert the needle back into the fabric above and to the right of the line to be covered. Keeping the thread beneath the needle, bring the needle up on the line, centered between the upper points. Passing the needle over the thread, insert it back into the fabric slightly below the line.

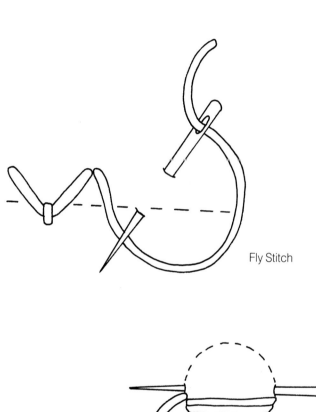

Fly Stitch

Satin Stitch

This stitch is used to cover areas like flowers, leaves, or facial features with stitches. It is made by filling in an area with closely spaced parallel stitches. Before stitching, draw an outline around the area to be covered, and then work within the guidelines.

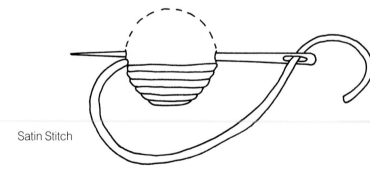

Satin Stitch

Stem Stitch

This stitch is used for sewing embroidery outlines. Beginning at the left end of the line to be covered, bring the needle up through the fabric to the right side. Insert the needle back into the fabric slightly to the right of the line. Bring the needle up halfway between these two points.

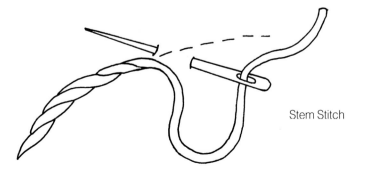

Stem Stitch

HOME AND HEARTH

◆ LONEFLOWER TABLECLOTH AND CHAIR PAD ◆

◆ *This classic blue-and-white tablecloth uses a patchwork technique called Seminole piecing. Named for the Seminole Indians of Florida, it is used here in its simplest form to create a basic checkerboard motif around an appliquéd center medallion.*

Seminole piecing can best be described as "strip piecing"; that is, strips of fabric are sewn together by machine, then cut into sections and resewn in many different ways to form designs. To eliminate bulkiness, no batting is used in this tablecloth. The backing and top piece are simply tied with embroidery floss.

The matching appliquéd and quilted chair pad will cushion a round or square seat. It is held in place by generous ties that can be made into bows around the chair back.

TABLECLOTH

SIZE: 71" × 71"

MATERIALS *Cotton fabrics:*
    2¼ yards 45"-wide dark-blue print
    2¼ yards 45"-wide light-blue print
4 yards 45"-wide white light-weight backing fabric
6-strand embroidery floss, 3 skeins matching dark blue
White sewing thread

See Enlarging Patterns, page 16. Enlarge petal pattern and cut from paper.

From dark-blue fabric mark, then cut six 6½" × 52" strips, four 6½" × 26" strips, two 3½" × 18½" strips, two 3½" × 24" strips and six petal pieces.

From light-blue fabric, mark and cut six 6½" × 52" strips, four 6½" × 26" strips and one 18½" × 18½" square center medallion.

All seams are ¼". With right sides together and alternating colors, machine-stitch long edges of 52" strips together. With right sides together and alternating colors, stitch two panels each of two dark-blue and two light-blue 26" strips. Press seams away from lighter color fabric.

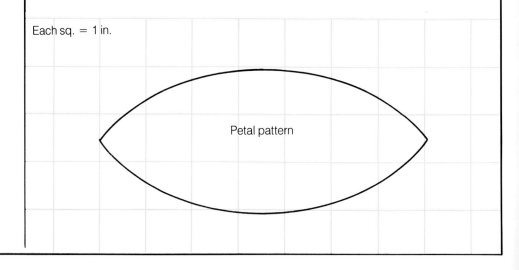

Each sq. = 1 in.

Petal pattern

28

Following Diagram A, place stitched panels right side up on flat surface. Measure and mark lines for eight equal 6½"-wide strips on 52" panel. Measure and mark lines for four equal 6½" strips on 26" panels. Cut each strip along lines.

Pin petals to 18½" square in Lone Flower motif. Turning edges under ¼" as you sew, slip-stitch into place. With right sides together, stitch 3½" × 18" strips across opposite sides of medallion. Press seams away from medallion. Stitch 3½" × 24" strips across unstitched medallion sides.

Following Diagram B, stitch fabric pieces together to make tablecloth top. To make tablecloth backing, cut backing fabric into two equal 2-yard pieces. Stitch pieces together along selvage edge. Press seams open.

Lay backing piece on flat surface. Measure 36" from center seam; trim excess fabric on both sides of backing piece. Finished backing will be 72" × 72" square.

With right sides together, pin tablecloth top to the backing fabric. Machine-stitch around outer edge, leaving 10" opening along one side for turning. Turn right side out, slip-stitch opening closed. Press edges of tablecloth.

Lay tablecloth on flat surface and pin layers together. See Tying Quilts, page 19. Using 6-strand embroidery floss, tie corners of each block. Leave ¾" end on each strand of floss.

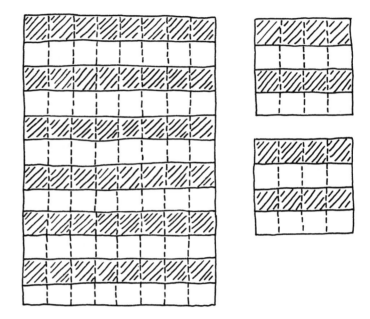

DIAGRAM A

DIAGRAM B

CHAIR PAD

SIZE: 15″ in diameter

MATERIALS   *Cotton fabrics:*
   *½ yard 45″-wide light-blue
      print*
   8″ × 22″ piece dark-blue print
   *16½″ × 16½″ square extra-loft
      quilt batting*
Sewing thread to match fabrics
White quilting thread

See Enlarging Patterns, page 16. Enlarge and cut petal pattern from Lone Flower Tablecloth.

From blue fabric cut six petals. From light-blue fabric mark with a compass, then cut two circles 16″ in diameter. Mark and cut four 3″ × 18″ strips.

To make ties for chair pad, press ¼″ along edges and one short edge of each 3″ × 18″ strip under ¼″. Press ties in half lengthwise so folded edges meet. Machine-top-stitch ⅛″ from fold. Lining up raw edges of ties with raw edge of one fabric circle, baste two sets of ties 8″ apart to right side of circle. See Diagram A.

Arrange six cut-out petals in Lone Flower motif on right side of remaining fabric circle (edges will overlap slightly before they are turned under). Turning edges under ¼″ as you sew, slip-stitch petals into place.

Place fabric circles right sides together with batting underneath. Machine-stitch circles with ¼″ seam, leaving 4″ opening for turning. Trim excess batting and turn right side out. Slip-stitch opening closed.

Baste chair-pad layers together from the center outward. Quilt inside appliqués ¼″ from fabric edge. Contour-quilt around outside of appliqués ¼″ from fabric edge. Quilt around perimeter of chair pad ½″ from edge.

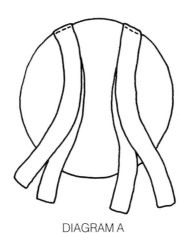

DIAGRAM A

◆ GRANDMOTHER'S FAN TABLECLOTH AND NAPKINS WITH SWEETHEART NAPKIN RINGS ◆

◆ *A charming design inspired by an old-fashioned "Grandmother's fan" patch-work block. The creamy-white quilted round tablecloth is appliquéd with the colorful fan motif. Appliqué hearts and a gathered ruffle complete the look.*

Each cloth napkin has a miniature

Grandmother's fan appliqué that has been stuffed lightly and quilted. The Sweet-heart Napkin Rings repeat the quilted heart motif of the tablecloth.

Whether used together or separately, this quilted ensemble is a delightful way to brighten any table.

FAN TABLECLOTH

SIZE: 68" in diameter

MATERIALS *Cotton fabrics:*
3½ yards 36"- or 45"-wide off-white
3½ yards 36"-wide muslin
1¼ yards 45"-wide yellow print
⅜ yard 45"-wide green print
¼ yard 45"-wide blue print
¼ yard 45"-wide pink print
65" × 65" piece quilt batting
Sewing thread to match off-white, green, and yellow fabrics
White quilting thread

See Enlarging Patterns, page 16. Enlarge and cut pattern pieces from paper. Letter A and B according to pattern diagram, page 34.

From green fabric cut four A pieces, two B pieces, and six hearts. From yellow, blue, and pink fabrics cut four A pieces each.

Cut 3½ yards off-white fabric into two equal 63" pieces. Machine-stitch pieces together lengthwise along one selvage edge. Press seam open. Repeat preceding step with muslin.

To cut off-white fabric into circle 62" in diameter, fold fabric in half along seam line as shown in Diagram A. Fold fabric in half again so short sides meet. Fold fabric so seamed edge meets folded edge, creating a 45-degree angle.

Fold 45-degree angle in half. Measure 31" from point of angle and place marks at 1" intervals along area. Connect marks to form an arc. Cut along arc line.

Open circle and lay flat. Starting from center of circle, measure and mark horizontal and vertical quilting lines 2" apart over entire circle piece.

All seams are ¼". With right sides together and stitching along straight sides, machine-stitch eight A pieces together; alternate fabrics. Stitch second panel of A pieces together in the same fabric order. Press seams open. With right sides together hand-baste, then machine-stitch curved edge of B pieces to stitched A pieces. Press edges of fan appliqués under ¼"

Center and pin fan appliqués to circle so bottom points of fans are 1" apart. Slip-stitch into place. Spacing heart appliqués equally around outside of circle, pin bottom of hearts 2" away from fabric edge. Turning edges under ⅛" as you sew, slip-stitch the hearts into place.

Following pattern diagram, trace

Each sq. = 1 in.

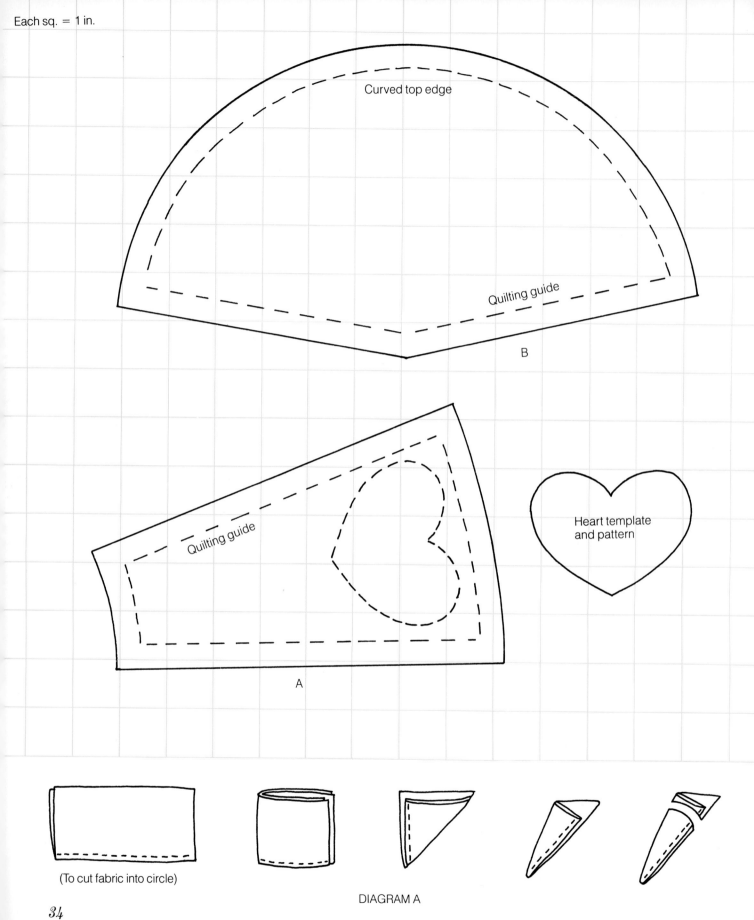

Curved top edge

Quilting guide

B

Quilting guide

A

Heart template
and pattern

(To cut fabric into circle)

DIAGRAM A

heart onto each A piece.

Sandwich batting between circle and muslin. Baste layers together. Quilting from the center outward, quilt around outside edges of appliqués ¼" from fabric edge. Quilt appliqués ¼" from all seams. Quilt over marked lines and heart shapes on fans.

Machine-zigzag around outside edge of quilted top piece. Trim excess batting and fabric.

To make the ruffle, mark and cut remaining yellow fabric into seven 5"×45" strips. Starting ½" from each end, run gathering stitch along one 45" side of each strip.

With right sides together, stitch strips together along 5" sides. Press seams open. Press bottom edge of strips under ¼" twice, then machine-hem.

With right sides together, line up raw edge of tablecloth with raw edge of ruffle and gather ruffle to fit tablecloth. Pin, than machine-stitch with ⅜" seam.

FAN NAPKIN

SIZE: 16"×16"

MATERIALS *Cotton fabrics:*
   17"×17" piece off-white
   3"×6" piece green print
   2½"×3" pieces pink, blue, and
      yellow prints
4"×5½" piece quilt batting
Off-white sewing thread
White quilting thread

Trace A and B patterns, then cut from paper.

Cut one A piece from green fabric. Cut one B piece from green, pink, blue, and yellow fabrics. All seams are ¼". With right sides together, stitch B pieces along straight sides. Hand-baste, then machine-stitch curved side of A

piece to B pieces. Press all edges under ¼".

Pin fan appliqué to batting. Trim excess batting. Press raw edges of off-white fabric under ¼" twice, then slip-stitch. With batting still in place, pin fan appliqué 1½" in from corner edge of one napkin. Using off-white thread, slip-stitch fan to napkin, pushing excess batting under appliqué. Quilt fan ¼" from outside edge and ¼" away from all seams.

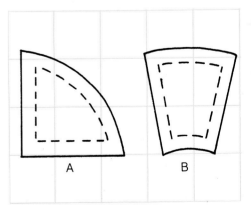

A   B

NAPKIN RING

SIZE: 2″ × 8″ in diameter

MATERIALS *For each napkin ring:*
6″ × 9″ piece cotton fabric
6½″ × 9½″ piece batting
Sewing thread to match fabric
White quilting thread

Trace heart template and cut from paper.

With wrong sides facing, fold fabric in half lengthwise so 9″ sides meet. Measure and mark ¼″ quilting line from top folded edge. Measure and mark ½″ quilting line from bottom raw edge. Leaving ¾″ seam allowance at each short end, center and trace three hearts onto fabric between top and bottom quilting lines.

Open fabric and baste batting to wrong side. With right sides together, fold fabric. Stitch along 9″ side with ¼″ seam. Trim batting and seam allowance to ⅛″. Turn right side out. Baste layers together. Leaving ¾″ seam allowance unquilted at each end, quilt over drawn lines. Quilt a second heart ¼″ inside center heart.

Trim ¼″ from one end of quilted ring. Trim corners slightly and insert shortened end of ring inside opposite end. Baste ring together ½″ from raw edge. Folding raw edge under ¼″ as you sew, slip-stitch ends of napkin ring together.

Heart template

◆ SPRING BLOSSOM PLACE MAT AND NAPKIN ◆

◆ *With this cheery place mat and napkin set, you will find yourself celebrating a sunny spring morning anytime of the year. It is especially nice in midwinter when you long to see bright blossoms.*

For the place mat, graceful pink and green flowers are appliquéd to a coordinating floral background and the entire piece is quilted. A single spring blossom is appliquéd to a corner of each cloth napkin. To achieve a delicately puffed, sculptured effect, the blossom is then stuffed and quilted.

Sunday brunch for two on the terrace? Duplicate your needlework efforts for twice the fun and twice the enjoyment.

PLACE MAT

SIZE: 11½″ × 16″

MATERIALS *For each place mat:*
  6″ × 8″ pieces green and dark pink cotton fabrics
  ⅓ yard background cotton fabric, 45″-wide
  1½ yards single-fold bias tape, or 1″-wide bias strip
  14″ × 18″ piece quilt batting
  White quilting thread
  Sewing thread to match fabrics

See Enlarging Patterns, page 16. Enlarge the patterns and cut from paper. Letter each pattern as shown in pattern diagram. Draw the appliqué outlines on A pattern, as indicated.

Cut one A piece from background fabric. Place A piece right side down on sheet of dressmaker's carbon paper. Place A pattern on top of fabric and trace over appliqué outlines with tracing wheel or sharp pencil.

Cut four B pieces from dark-pink fabric and four C pieces from green fabric. Cut two D and E pieces each from green fabric.

Pin B, C, D, and E pieces into place on A and slip-stitch; turn edges under ⅛″ with thumb and forefinger as you sew. Draw diagonal quilting lines 2″ apart on appliquéd top piece.

Sandwich quilt batting between A piece and 12½″ × 17″ piece of background fabric. Baste layers together, working from center outward. Quilt, following traced lines and stitching inside the appliqué pieces, ⅛″ from the edge. Machine-zigzag along edge of top piece. Trim away excess batting and fabric.

See Binding Edges, page 20. Bind edge of place mat with ¼″ seam allowance.

Each sq. = 1 in.

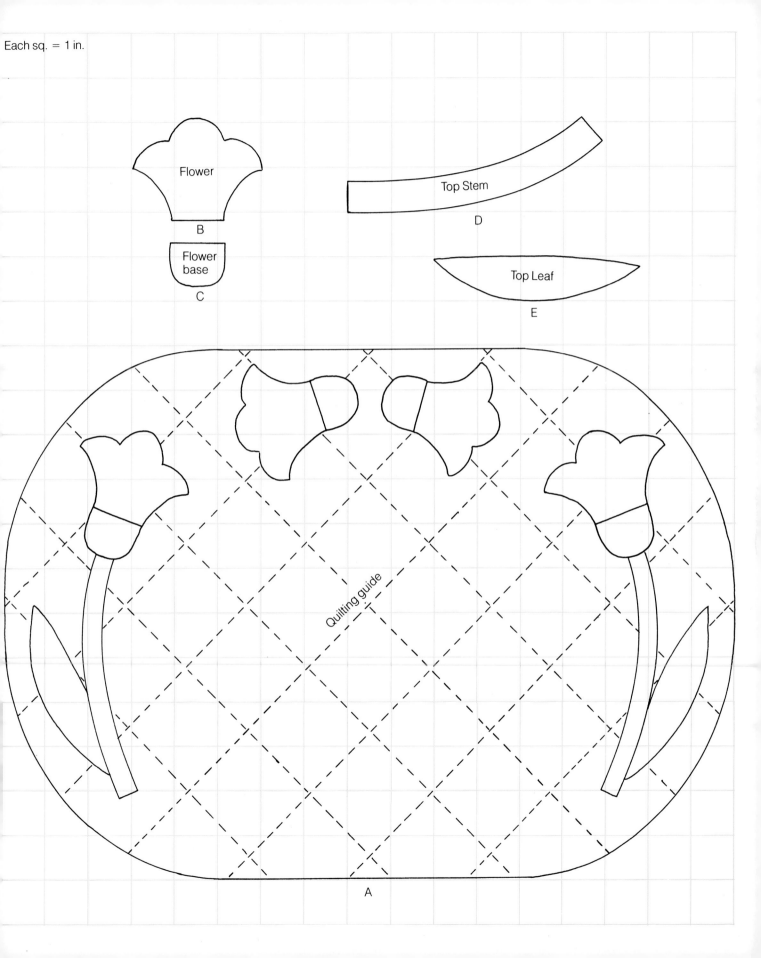

Flower

B

Top Stem

D

Flower
base

C

Top Leaf

E

Quilting guide

A

NAPKIN

SIZE: 17″ × 17″

MATERIALS *For each napkin:*
   18″ × 18″ piece off-white cotton fabric
   1½″ × 1½″ piece green cotton fabric
   3″ × 3½″ piece dark-pink cotton fabric
   Small scrap quilt batting
   Off-white sewing thread
   White quilting thread

Using B and C patterns from Spring Blossom Place Mat, cut one B from dark-pink and one C from green fabric.

Press edges of off-white fabric under ¼″ twice, then slip-stitch. With right sides together, stitch B to C along straight sides with ⅛″ seam allowance.

Using off-white thread and folding edges under ⅛″ as you sew, slip-stitch appliqué to napkin 2″ in from corner edge. Leave a 1″ opening along one side for stuffing.

With knitting needle or some other pointed object, stuff small pieces of quilt batting into appliqué opening. Stitch opening closed. Contour-quilt inside appliqué ¼″ from edge.

◆ AUTUMN-LEAF PLACE MAT AND NAPKIN ◆

◆ *In this project all the fiery yellows, reds, and oranges of autumn combine to reflect nature's splendor. The autumn-leaf shape is an easy-to-do technique called quilted counterpane. The leaf motif is the same on both sides of the place mat. It can be made reversible by using contrasting fabric for the backing. The matching cloth napkin has a small leaf appliquéd to one corner. It is lightly stuffed and quilted to create a three-dimensional effect.*

Easy to make, these place mats and napkins would be excellent bazaar best-sellers. Or make a place mat and napkin for a shut-in elderly friend or relative to brighten a dinner-for-one.

PLACE MAT

SIZE: 12″ × 18″

MATERIALS *For each place mat:*
½ yard 45″-wide yellow-print cotton fabric
14″ × 20″ piece extra-loft quilt batting
1½ yards single-fold bias tape
Quilting thread
Sewing thread to match fabric

See Enlarging Patterns, page 16. Enlarge leaf pattern and template, then cut from paper.

From fabric cut one leaf and one 14″ × 20″ rectangle. Following quilting guide (broken lines) on pattern diagram, trace template onto fabric leaf.

Mark a line through center of leaf and center of each traced template.

Sandwich quilt batting between leaf and fabric rectangle. Baste layers together. Quilt over traced lines. Zigzag-stitch along outside edge of leaf. Trim excess fabric and batting.

See Binding Edges, page 20. Bind around outside edge of leaf with bias tape, binding stem end first with 5″ piece of tape.

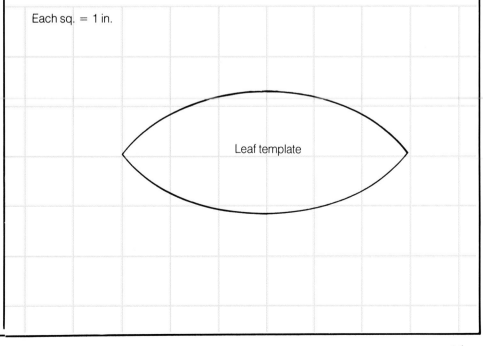

Each sq. = 1 in.

Leaf template

Each sq. = 1 in.

Quilting guide

Autumn-Leaf Place Mat pattern

NAPKIN

SIZE: 17" × 17"

MATERIALS *For each napkin:*
- *18" × 18" piece off-white cotton fabric*
- *3½" × 4" scrap yellow-print cotton fabric*
- *3½" × 4" piece extra-loft quilt batting*
- *Quilting thread*
- *Off-white sewing thread*

Trace leaf pattern and cut from paper. Press edges of off-white fabric under ¼" twice, then slip-stitch.

Cut one leaf from both print fabric and batting. Pin leaf to napkin so stem end is 2" in from one corner. Using off-white thread and small, regular stitches, slip-stitch leaf to napkin; turn leaf edges under ⅛" as you sew. Leave 2" opening on one side. Insert batting between napkin and leaf appliqué. Stitch opening closed. Following pattern guide, quilt leaf appliqué.

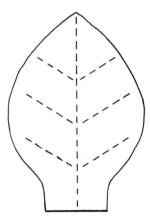

Leaf pattern for napkin

◆ PINEAPPLE-PERFECT TRAY PAD ◆

◆ *The pineapple is a traditional symbol of warmth and welcome…and the motif occupies a strong place in American quilting, stenciling, and furniture design.*

The pad shown here was made for a rectangular tray that measures 14″ × 18″. But you can make it in other sizes and shapes to fit an heirloom or contemporary tray. The subdued calico background of pastel purples and off-white contrasts with the bold yellow, purple, and green of the pineapples. Try other color combinations for a different effect—yellows, blues, and pinks would be just as attractive.

SIZE: 13″ × 17″ (fits 14″ × 18″ tray)

This pad can be made to fit a tray of any size. Measure inside length and width of tray and add 1″ to each measurement. The pineapple motif can be enlarged or reduced, following directions on Enlarging Patterns, page 16. Be sure to increase or reduce binding and piping strips proportionately.

MATERIALS *Cotton fabrics:*
½ yard 45″-wide white print
9″ × 21″ piece purple print
7½″ × 15″ piece solid green
7″ × 21″ piece solid yellow
15″ × 19″ piece extra-loft quilt batting
Quilting thread
Sewing thread to match fabrics
14″ × 18″ tray

See Enlarging Patterns, page 16. Enlarge pattern pieces and cut from paper.

From purple print mark and cut one large pineapple, two 2″ × 17″ binding strips, and two 2″ × 15″ binding strips on straight grain of fabric.

From yellow fabric mark and cut two small pineapples, two 1½″ × 17″ piping strips, and two 1½″ × 13″ piping strips on straight grain of fabric.

From green fabric cut two leaves, two small pineapple tops, one large pineapple top, one 1″ × 3½″ stem and two 1″ × 4″ stems.

Following pattern diagram, draw quilting lines on pineapples.

From white print cut one 14″ × 18″ rectangle. Following Diagram A, arrange appliqués on rectangle.

Pin, then slip-stitch into place, turning edges under ⅛″ as you sew.

Cut a 15″ × 19″ rectangle from white print. Sandwich quilt batting between rectangles. Baste layers together, stitching from center outwards.

Quilt pineapples, following marked lines. Quilt ¼″ inside remaining appliqué shapes.

Contour quilt ¼″ outside of each appliqué shape. Continue contour quilting at ½″ intervals until entire background is quilted.

Zigzag stitch along outside edge of appliquéd rectangle. Checking pad measurements before you cut fabric, trim excess batting and fabric.

Press yellow piping strips in half lengthwise. Lining up the raw edges, baste piping to outside edge of pad, overlapping piping on corners.

See Binding Edges, page 20.

Using ½″ seams, bind the long sides of tray pad with 17″ strips and short sides with the 15″ strips.

46

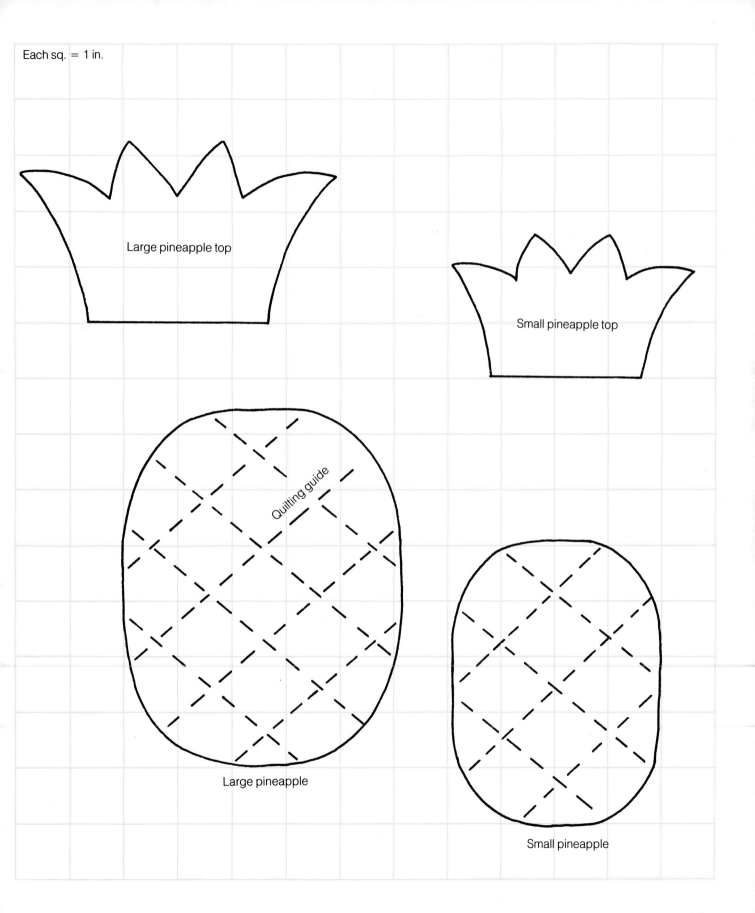

Each sq. = 1 in.

Large pineapple top

Small pineapple top

Quilting guide

Large pineapple

Small pineapple

47

Each sq. = 1 in.

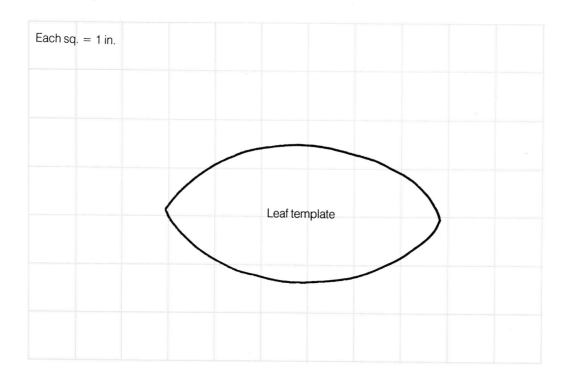

Leaf template

DIAGRAM A

◆ NATURE'S BOUNTY COASTERS ◆

◆ *Coasters are as basic to summer as the sound of screendoors slamming shut…or the tinkle of ice in a pitcher of lemonade. This unique set of coasters features a luscious variety of fresh fruits-of-the-season embroidered on unbleached muslin. The* *designs are then quilted and encircled by eyelet lace to create beautiful coasters that can be used all summer under frosty glasses. These fruit motifs can also be used on other household items, such as place mats, pillows, or pot holders.*

SIZE: 5″ in diameter

MATERIALS

¼ yard 36″-wide unbleached muslin
2¼ yards 1″-wide gathered eyelet lace
9″ × 14″ piece quilt batting
6-strand embroidery floss:
  2 yards green, brown, and orange
  3 yards red and yellow
White sewing thread
White quilting thread

Trace and draw embroidery patterns on paper, allowing 3″ between each design. Using a compass, draw a circle 4″ in diameter. Cut out paper circle and trace on muslin six times.

Center and place each embroidery drawing under muslin circle. Trace designs directly onto fabric. Do not cut out circles.

See Embroidery Stitches, page 22. Using stem stitch, embroider each fruit drawing. Leaves are green, stems are brown, and fruit is corresponding color (see photograph). Cut out each circle.

Divide lace into six 13½″ pieces. Lining up raw edge of circle with top (gathered) edge of lace, machine-baste lace to right side of each circle with ⅛″ seam.

From muslin and batting, cut six 4½″ × 4½″ squares each. Place muslin squares right sides together with circles. Pin batting under squares. Machine-stitch around outside edge of circles with ¼″ seam, leaving 2″ opening for turning. Trim excess batting and muslin.

Turn circles right side out and slip-stitch opening closed. Quilt each coaster ¼″ from outside edge and contour-quilt around each embroidered design ⅛″ from stitches.

To make coasters waterproof, spray with Scotchgard®.

Each sq. = 1 in.

Apple

Pear

Lemon

Pineapple

Strawberry

Cherry

♦ CALICO BASKET LINER ♦

♦ *For a hearty country breakfast, serve freshly baked corn muffins and date-nut bread in a basket lined with this calico liner. Fast and easy to make, the Calico Basket Liner is machine-quilted and stitched…and it can be made to fit any flat-bottomed basket without handles.*

Make yours from the same printed fabric used in other kitchen/dining-room accessories—or sew up a batch in "new" colors, like Memphis mint, perfect peach, or Santa Fe pink.

SIZE: Any medium-size basket, approximately 4″ high × 9″ in diameter.

MATERIALS

½ yard cotton fabric

1½″-wide eyelet lace measuring circumference of basket top plus 2″

Extra-loft quilt batting, approximately 7″ × 38″

White quilting thread

Basket

To make pattern for basket bottom, trace bottom of basket onto paper. Add ¼″ all around and cut out. Cut one basket bottom from fabric.

Mark vertical quilting lines 1″ apart on right side of fabric. From both fabric and quilt batting, cut one basket bottom ½″ larger than pattern. Sandwich batting between fabric pieces. Pin the layers together. Starting from center quilting line, machine-quilt over the drawn lines. Zigzag-stitch around outside edge of smaller fabric piece. Trim excess fabric and batting.

To make a rectangle, measure height of basket plus 1½″ by circumference of basket top plus 2″. Cut one rectangle from fabric and mark vertical quilting lines 1″ apart on right side of fabric. Cut another slightly larger rectangle from both fabric and batting.

Press one long side of each fabric rectangle under ¼″. Sandwich batting between fabric rectangles, lining up folded edges of fabric with edge of batting. Baste layers together, stopping 1″ from folded edges.

Stitching close to folded edge of fabric, pin, then machine-top-stitch, eyelet lace inside opening between fabric rectangles. Machine-quilt over marked quilted lines. Zigzag-stitch around outside edge of smaller rectangle. Trim the excess fabric and batting.

With right sides together, stitch side seam with ¼″ seam. Pin, then hand-baste stitched rectangle to quilted bottom piece; gather the excess fabric evenly as you sew. Machine-stitch over basting with ¼″ seam. Slip basket liner inside basket, folding top edge over basket sides.

REST EASY

◆ COUNTRY BISCUITS PILLOW ◆

◆ *A real first-prize winner! To achieve the desired effect, small fabric puffs are stuffed and stitched together. This is then topped off by frilly eyelet edging, which adds a note of old-time charm.*

The pillow shown here is made of both a light and a dark pastel print, the coordi-nating colors creating a unique checker-board of light and dark puffs. But don't stop there—use your imagination and try other color combinations.

This project boasts a classic, time-tested design that any serious quilter will find impossible to resist.

SIZE: 15″ × 15″

MATERIALS *Cotton fabrics:*
   ½ yard 45″-wide dark print
   ¼ yard 45″-wide light print
   ¼ yard 45″-wide backing fabric, (muslin or any lightweight cotton fabric)
1¾ yards gathered eyelet lace, 2¾″ wide
12 oz. polyester stuffing
Sewing thread to match fabrics

With a ruler and a pencil, mark off and cut thirty-six 3″ squares from backing fabric. Cut one 16″ × 16″ square and eighteen 4″ squares from dark print. Cut eighteen 4″ squares from light print.

Pin corners of each 4″ print square to corners of a 3″ backing square. See Diagram A. In center of each side fold and pin excess fabric into pleats, folding all pleats in the same direction.

Before pinning fourth side, insert small handful of polyester stuffing into opening. See Diagram B. Baste around edges of each square. See Diagram C.

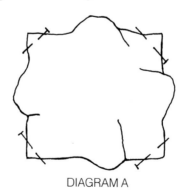

DIAGRAM A

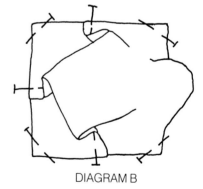

DIAGRAM B

DIAGRAM C

Machine-stitch biscuits together in rows of six, using ¼" seams and alternating colors. Start and end three rows with dark-print biscuits and three rows with light-print biscuits. Carefully press seams open. Stitch rows together with ¼" seams, alternating light and dark biscuits. Press seams open.

Lining up raw edge of stitched biscuits with bottom edge of lace, baste lace into place around outside edge of stitched biscuits.

With right sides together pin, then machine-stitch 16" × 16" piece of dark-print fabric to stitched biscuits with ¼" seams. Leave a 7" opening along one side.

Turn pillow right side out. Fill with polyester stuffing. Slip-stitch opening closed and raw ends of lace together.

◆ SEA TREASURE PILLOWS ◆

◆ *Plump and imaginative pillows always look inviting, whether they're on an easy chair by the fireplace or placed casually on a deacon's bench in the breezeway.*

The design for these pillows was inspired by the shapes of beautiful shells on Cape Cod's beaches. The appliquéd designs are handsomely set off by the soft, quilted shapes and contrasting fabrics.

SEA SHELL PILLOW

SIZE: 17″ × 17″

MATERIALS *Cotton fabrics:*
½ yard 45″-wide print
10″ × 11″ piece print
2½″ × 3½″ piece solid
19″ × 19″ piece muslin or any lightweight backing fabric
19″ × 19″ and 10″ × 11″ pieces extra-loft quilt batting
12 oz. polyester stuffing
White quilting thread
Sewing thread to match fabrics

See Enlarging Patterns, page 16. Enlarge pattern pieces and cut from paper. Letter each pattern as shown in diagram. Draw quilting guide (broken lines) and appliqué placement lines on A and B.

Cut one A and one C piece from ½-yard print fabric. Cut one B piece from 10″ × 11″ piece of fabric and one D piece from solid fabric. Place A and B right sides down on dressmaker's carbon paper. Place A and B patterns on top of fabric and trace over quilting and appliqué lines with a sharp pencil.

Baste edges of B under ¼″. Press edges of C and D pieces under ¼″. Clip excess fabric at points. Pin, then slip-stitch D into place on C, and C into place on B.

Cut B piece from 10″ × 11″ quilt batting and baste it to wrong side of B fabric piece. Baste, then slip-stitch B onto A, pushing any excess quilt batting under B. Quilt B appliqué, following traced quilting lines.

Sandwich 19″ × 19″ quilt batting between top A piece and 19″ × 19″ backing fabric. Baste from center outward and quilt, following traced lines. Around perimeter of A, baste permanently ⅛″ in from edge. Trim excess backing fabric and quilt batting.

With right sides together, pin quilted A top piece to remaining print fabric. Machine-stitch around A with ¼″ seam, leaving 4″ opening along bottom. Trim excess fabric and clip curves.

Turn right side out and fill with polyester stuffing. Slip-stitch opening closed.

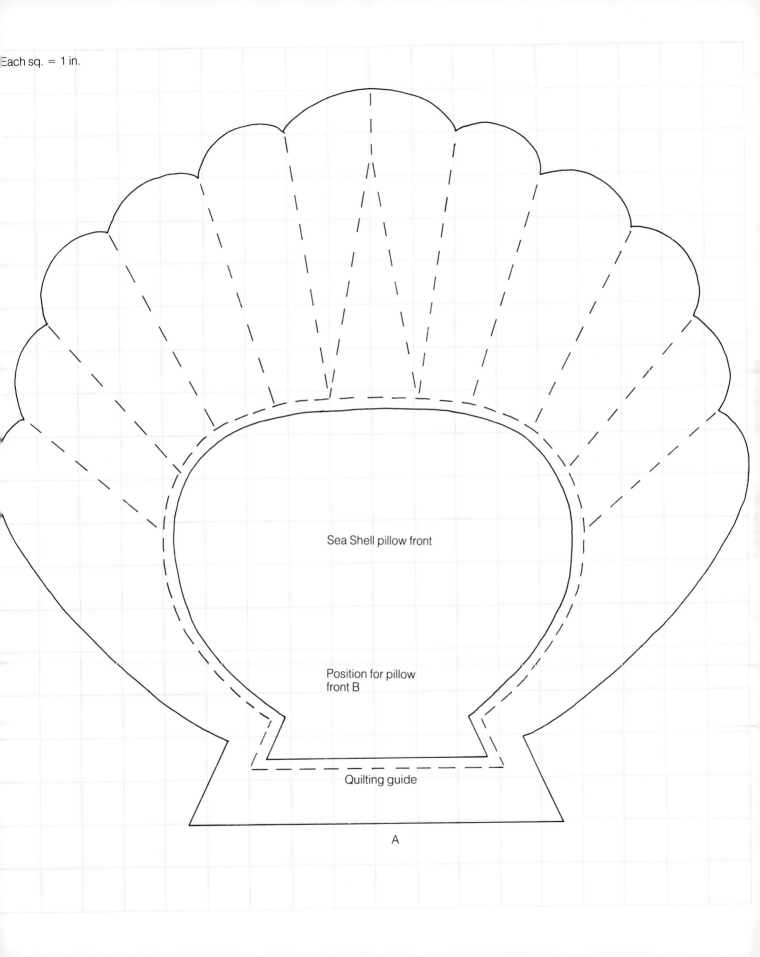

Each sq. = 1 in.

Sea Shell pillow front

Position for pillow
front B

Quilting guide

A

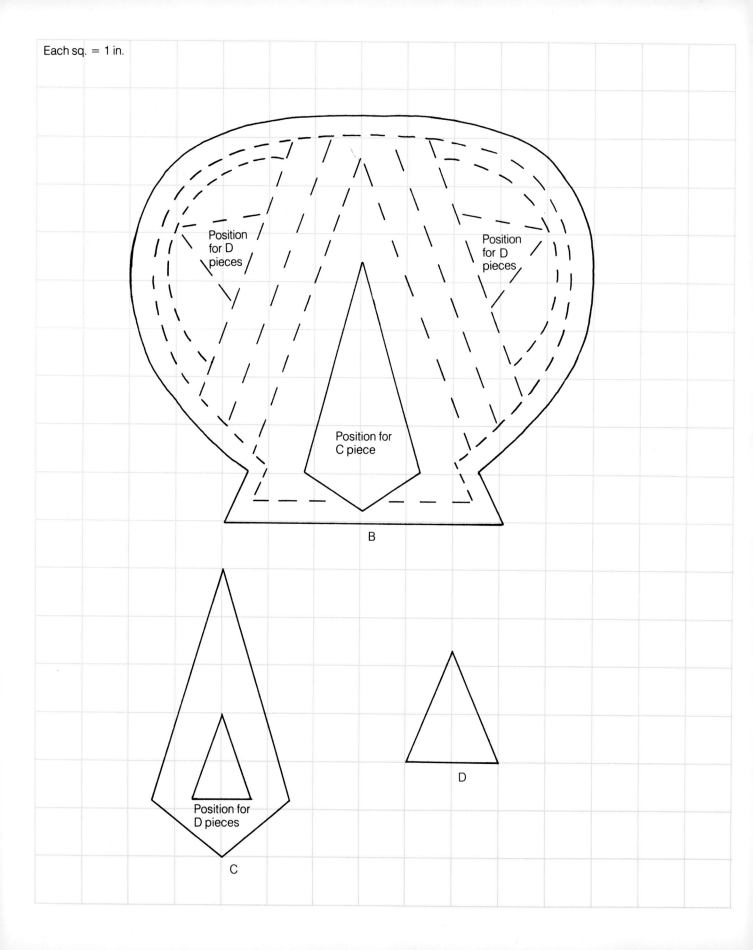

Each sq. = 1 in.

Position for D pieces

Position for D pieces

Position for C piece

B

Position for D pieces

C

D

SEA GEM PILLOW

SIZE: 17″ × 17″

MATERIALS *Cotton fabrics:*
½ yard 45″-wide print
9″ × 10″ piece red
10″ × 12″ piece yellow
18″ × 19″ piece muslin or any lightweight backing fabric
18″ × 19″ and 9″ × 10″ pieces extra-loft quilt batting
12 oz. polyester stuffing
White quilting thread
Sewing thread to match fabrics

See Enlarging Patterns, page 16. Enlarge pattern pieces and cut from paper. Letter each pattern according to diagram. Draw quilting guide (broken lines) and appliqué placement lines on A and B.

Cut one A and D piece each from print fabric, and one B piece from red fabric. Cut six C pieces from yellow fabric. Place A and B fabric pieces right sides down on dressmaker's carbon paper. Place A and B patterns on top of fabric and trace over quilting and appliqué placement lines with a sharp pencil.

Baste edges of B and D pieces under ¼″. Press two long sides of C pieces under ¼″, leaving bottom side unpressed. Clip excess fabric at center point. Pin, then slip-stitch the C pieces into place on A. Pin, then slip-stitch D into place on B.

Cut a B piece from 9″ × 10″ quilt batting and baste it to wrong side of B fabric piece. Baste, then slip-stitch B onto A; push any excess quilt batting under B. Quilt B appliqué, following traced quilting lines.

Sandwich 18″ × 19″ piece of quilt batting between top A piece and 18″ × 19″ backing fabric. Baste from center outward and quilt, following traced lines. Around the perimeter of A, baste permanently ⅛″ in from edge. Trim excess backing fabric and quilt batting.

With right sides together, pin quilted A top piece to remaining print fabric. Machine-stitch around A with ¼″ seam, leaving 4″ opening along bottom. Trim excess fabric and clip curves.

Turn right side out and fill with polyester stuffing. Slip-stitch opening closed.

Each sq. = 1 in.

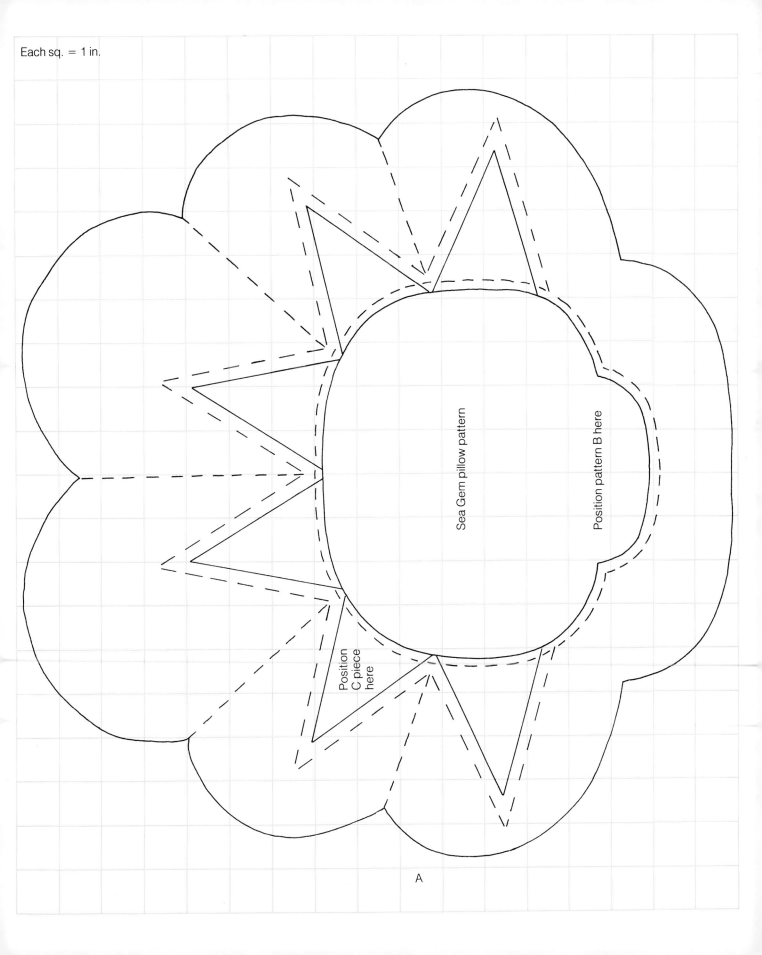

Sea Gem pillow pattern

Position pattern B here

Position
C piece
here

A

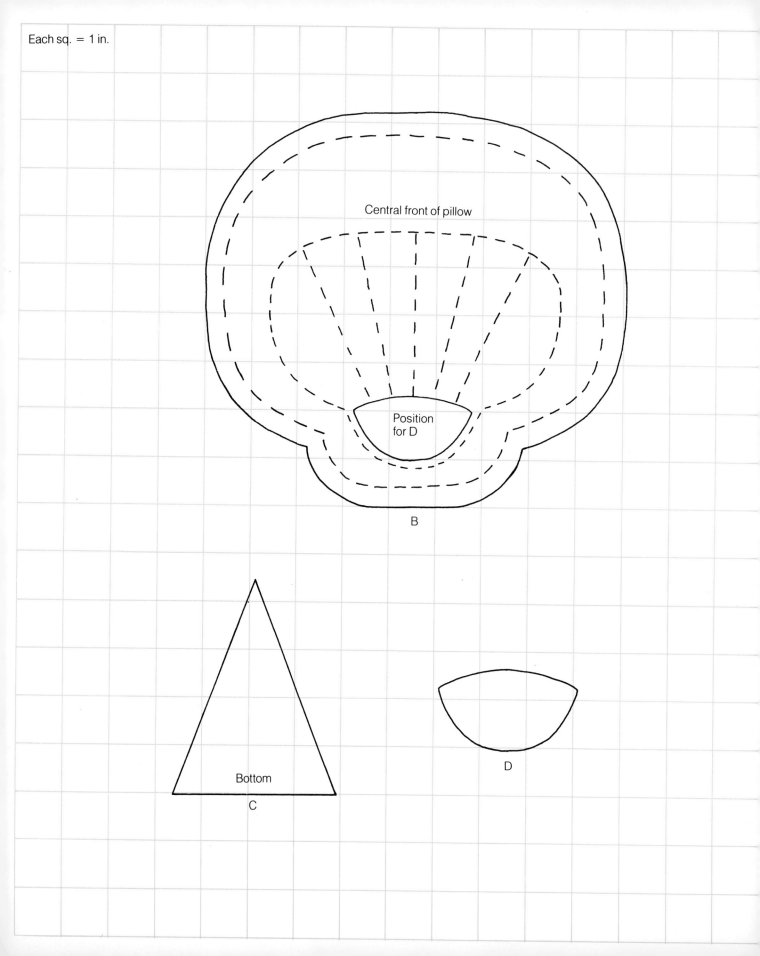

Each sq. = 1 in.

Central front of pillow

Position
for D

B

Bottom

C

D

◆ NORTH STAR PATCHWORK PILLOW ◆

◆ *Star patterns can be found on American quilts as early as the 17th century.*

Patchwork stars were sewn in an endless array of patterns — everything from single-star designs to motifs in which hundreds of tiny diamond-shapes were stitched together to form a large central medallion. Whether simple or complex, the star pattern is always impressive.

The North Star Pillow is an easy project in which light and dark contrasting diamond shapes are stitched together, then surrounded by diamond shapes in a contrasting solid or calico print. Your North Star Pillow is sure to attract attention and admiration.

SIZE: 17½″ × 20″ at widest diagonal

MATERIALS *Cotton fabrics:*
   ¼ yard light print and dark print
   ½ yard dark contrasting print or solid color
   19″ × 22″ piece white muslin
   19″ × 22″ piece extra-loft quilt batting
16 oz. polyester stuffing
Off-white quilting thread
Sewing thread to match fabrics

Trace and cut diamond pattern from paper. From both light- and dark-print fabrics, cut three diamonds. Cut six diamonds from contrasting fabric. Mark A and B sides of print diamonds with a pin. These are inner edges that will be joined to form the star. (The point where A and B meet is the center point of the star.)

All seam allowances are ¼″. With right sides together and carefully matching center points, machine-stitch A and B sides of the diamonds; alternate light and dark fabrics. Leave ¼″ unstitched at each end of seams to make piecing easier. Press all seams away from light-print fabric.

Mark D sides of contrasting diamonds with a pin. With right sides together, machine-stitch D sides of contrasting diamonds to C sides of print diamonds. See Diagram A for placement. When you reach the center angle, place sewing-machine needle all the way down into bobbin case, lift presser foot, turn fabric, and continue sewing. Press all seams away from light fabric.

Sandwich quilt batting between stitched diamond top piece and an 18″ × 21″ piece of muslin fabric, making sure that entire top piece is underlaid by muslin piece. Working from the center outward, baste all three layers together. Quilt inside each diamond ⅜″ from the seam, then quilt around perimeter of the entire top piece ⅝″ from the raw edge. Machine-zigzag around the outside edge of top piece. Trim excess batting and fabric.

Cut an 18″ × 21″ piece of contrasting fabric for pillow back. With the right sides together pin, then machine-stitch pillow top to pillow back. Leave 4″ unstitched along one side for stuffing.

Turn pillow right side out and stuff. Slip-stitch opening closed.

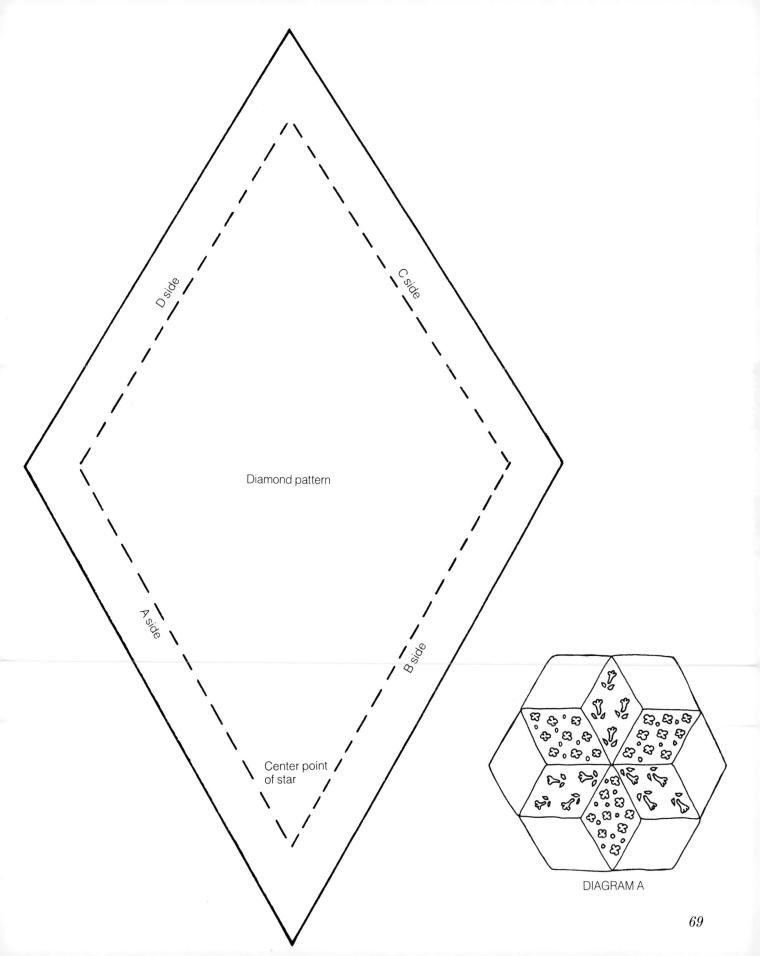

D side

C side

A side

B side

Diamond pattern

Center point
of star

DIAGRAM A

69

◆ BIRDS-IN-FLIGHT EXERCISE OR BEACH MAT ◆

◆ *For a total-body stretch workout or yoga, or for suntanning at the beach, this portable quilted mat is the ultimate in cushiony comfort. Afterward, just fold it* *into a compact roll and carry it along. The medium-weight cotton backing fabric is combined with machine quilting to provide added strength and durability.*

SIZE: 35" × 62"

MATERIALS *Cotton fabrics:*
2 yards 45"-wide medium-weight blue
½ yard 45"-wide maroon
1¾ yards 45"-wide off-white print
36" × 64" piece extra-loft quilt batting
Sewing thread to match fabrics
White quilting thread

See Enlarging Patterns, page 16. Enlarge bird pattern and cut from paper.

From off-white fabric, cut one 30" × 58" center panel and two 3" × 20" straps. From maroon fabric, cut two 4" × 30" strips and two bird pieces. From blue fabric, cut one 44" × 64" piece backing fabric and one bird piece.

Measuring 6½" from top and bottom (30" sides) of center panel, center and pin maroon birds into place with both birds facing in the same direction. Facing it in the opposite direction, center and pin blue bird between maroon birds. Turning edges under ¼" as you sew, slip-stitch bird appliqués into place.

All seams are ½". With right sides together, machine-stitch maroon strips across top and bottom of center panel. Press seams open. With right sides together, machine-stitch 64" sides of backing fabric to long sides of center panel. Press seams open.

Keeping it wrong side out, lay mat on flat surface with front panel facing up. The backing fabric is larger than the front panel. Pin fabric so the backing fabric creates a 3½" border on each side of center panel.

Center batting on top of fabric. Pin, then machine-stitch across bottom edge of mat, catching batting as you sew. Turn mat right side out, smoothing batting with a yardstick so it lies evenly inside mat and blue borders remain 3½" wide. Baste layers together, leaving top edge open.

Press all edges of straps under ¼". Press straps lengthwise so folded edges meet. Machine-top-stitch ⅛" from folded strap edges. Fold each strap in half. Lining up fold with raw edge of fabric, baste straps to seam allowance along top edge of mat 12" from each side. Fold raw edges along the top opening under ½". Slip-stitch opening closed.

See Machine-Quilting, page 18. Machine-quilt center panel ⅛" from outside edge and ⅛" from outside edge of bird appliqués. Following Diagram A, mark, then machine-quilt randomly placed wavy horizontal lines, filling center panel. Machine-quilt around perimeter of mat ⅜" from edge.

To fold the mat into a compact roll, fold both long sides in toward the center approximately 10". Start rolling the strapless end towards the straps, then tie straps around the roll.

Each sq. = 1 in.

Bird pattern

DIAGRAM A

♦ CALICO CACTUS PLANTER ♦

♦ A cactus would certainly be in its element in this planter. It's also an ideal way to show off a centerpiece of wildflowers, or an intriguing arrangement of dried flowers, or even a potted plant.

For quick-and-easy construction, Seminole piecing is the technique used in this project. Embroidery floss ties simulate the spiky ends of a cactus. And any combination of contrasting fabrics can be used to achieve a checker-board effect. For a Christmas poinsettia, try a red and green combination. It makes a bright gift for the holidays.

SIZE: 7½" in height

MATERIALS *Cotton fabrics:*
  5" × 28" piece blue print
  6½" × 28" and 8" × 8" pieces dark-pink print
  9" × 24" and 8" × 8" pieces muslin or any lightweight backing fabric
9" × 24" piece quilt batting
Matching blue 6-strand embroidery floss
Sewing thread to match pink fabric
Empty plastic Clorox® bottle, 1-gallon size (optional)

Cut two 2¼" × 28" strips each from blue and pink print fabrics. Machine-stitch strips together lengthwise with ¼" seam, alternating colors. Press seam allowances open.

Place stitched strips right sides up on a flat surface. Carefully measure and mark eight equal 3¼"-wide strips. Cut each strip. See Diagram A. Turn every other strip upside down to create a checkerboard. Lining up seams carefully, machine-stitch strips together with ¼" seam. See Diagram B. Press all seam allowances open.

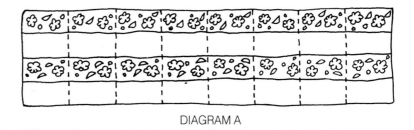

DIAGRAM A

DIAGRAM B

Sandwich quilt batting between backing fabric and top piece. Pin layers together. Using double strand of embroidery floss and leaving ½" at the end of each, tie corners of each block. See Tying Quilts, page 19.

Machine-zigzag around perimeter of tied top piece, stitching along edge of fabric. Trim excess quilt batting and backing fabric. With right sides together, machine-stitch side seam with ¼" seam. Tie corners along seam.

Draw a 7" circle on paper. Cut out and use as pattern for planter bottom. Cut one circle each from pink print and backing fabric. Machine-baste circles together ⅛" in from edge.

With right sides together pin, then machine-stitch circle to bottom edge of planter with ½" seam, gathering planter fabric slightly to fit. Turn planter right side out.

Cut 1½" × 25" strip of pink print fabric and seam-bind top edge of planter with a ¼" seam. See Binding Edges, page 20. Cut Clorox® bottle down to 6½" in height. Slip bottle into the planter to protect it from any water leakage.

COZY KITCHEN

◆ BABUSHKA TEA COZY ◆

◆ *A Babushka Tea Cozy to keep your tea piping hot! Bright and cheery, it's appliquéd and quilted to look like a Russian nesting doll. Her face is embroidered with a perpetual smile that makes teatime warm and friendly.*

Babushka is fun to make—and with doll-size porcelain teacups, even small children can enjoy the teatime ritual. (Half strength, please.)

It will make everything more cheerful on a rainy day.

SIZE: 10″ × 13″ (fits a 6- to 8-cup teapot)

MATERIALS *Cotton fabrics:*
   18″ × 24″ piece dark-pink print
   15″ × 24″ piece backing fabric
   6″ × 8½″ light blue
   6″ × 11″ yellow
   4″ × 4″ off-white
Two 12″ × 15″ pieces extra-loft quilt batting
White quilting thread
6-strand embroidery floss: 1 yard each dark pink and blue 2 yards black
4″ × 4″ piece fusible interacing
Sewing thread to match fabrics

See Enlarging Patterns, page 16. Enlarge pattern pieces and cut from paper. Letter each pattern according to diagram. Draw facial features on B.

From dark-pink print, cut two A pattern pieces and two 1″ × 14″ strips to be used as seam binding. Cut one B pattern piece from both off-white fabric and fusible interfacing. With hot iron, adhere interfacing to fabric. Place B right side down on dressmaker's carbon paper. Place B pattern on top and trace around facial features.

See Embroidery Stitches, page 22. Backstitch eyebrows, nose, and eye outlines with black embroidery floss. Fill in eyes and mouth with a satin stitch (mouth pink, irises blue, and pupils black). Turn under ¼″ around outer edge of B and baste.

Measure 1″ down from the top center of A. Pin B to A. Slip-stitch into place.

From blue fabric, cut one C piece and two D pieces. From yellow fabric, cut two C pieces and one E piece. Press two sides of the C pieces under ¼″, leaving bottom unpressed. Baste edges of D and E under ¼″. Following solid lines on pattern diagram, pin C, D, and E pieces into place on A and slip-stitch.

Sandwich a piece of quilt batting between appliquéd A piece and a 12″ × 15″ piece of backing fabric. Baste layers together. Contour-quilt around appliqués ¼″ beyond edges. Quilt inside contours of appliqués ¼″ in from edges. Measuring ½″ in from the raw edge, quilt around perimeter of A. Sandwich a piece of quilt batting between remaining A piece and fabric backing. Baste the layers together. Quilt around perimeter ½″ in from raw edges. Fill in background with vertically stitched quilting lines spaced 1″ apart. Baste around perimeter of both A pieces ⅛″ in from the edge. Trim excess quilt batting and fabric.

With right sides together, machine-stitch around outside edge of tea cozy with ¼″ seam allowance; leave bottom open. Turn cozy right side out.

See Binding Edges, page 20. Bind bottom edge with 1″ × 14″ strips of pink print.

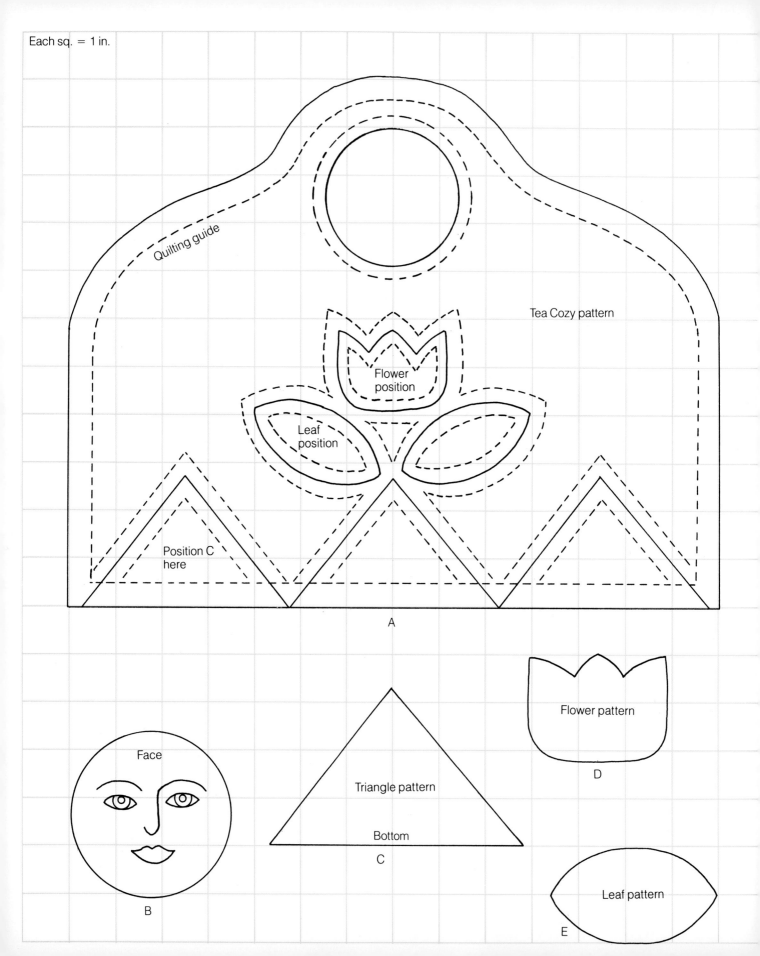

Each sq. = 1 in.

Quilting guide

Tea Cozy pattern

Flower position

Leaf position

Position C here

A

Face

B

Triangle pattern

Bottom

C

Flower pattern

D

Leaf pattern

E

◆ PINWHEEL POT HOLDER ◆

◆ *The patchwork motif of the Pinwheel Pot Holder is made by piecing together four smaller square patches (that's why the block is called "four-patch").*

Basic four-patch patterns are made up of four small blocks that are stitched together to form one larger block. By experimenting with the placement of the blocks, you can create many new designs simply by altering the arrangement.

The use of contrasting red and blue print fabrics is the key to the liveliness of the design. But any sharply contrasting fabrics can be used to achieve similar results. Seasonal colors can be fun: red and green for Christmas…pink and green for spring…yellow and red for autumn… lime-green and orange for summer.

SIZE: *7″ × 7″*

MATERIALS *Cotton fabrics:*
  10″ × 14″ piece print or plain
  5″ × 10″ piece print or plain
Two 9″ × 9″ squares quilt batting
1 yard single-fold bias tape or 1″-wide bias strip
White quilting thread
Sewing thread to match fabric

Trace and cut pattern from paper. Cut out four triangles each from both fabrics. On a flat surface, arrange the triangles in the pinwheel design. See Diagram A.

All seam allowances are ¼″. With right sides together, machine-stitch triangles together along diagonal to form four small squares. Press seam allowances away from the lighter colored fabric. Machine-stitch four small squares together to form one large square. See Diagram B. Press seam allowances away from lighter colored fabric.

Cut an 8″ × 8″ square from remaining piece of 10″ × 14″ fabric.

Sandwich two layers of quilt batting between square and top piece. Baste layers together and quilt inside each triangle ¼″ from the seams. Baste around edge of pot holder ⅛″ in from edge. Trim excess quilt batting and backing fabric. Curve corners slightly, taking care not to cut through the quilt stitching.

See Binding Edges, page 20. Starting on one corner, bind edge of pot holder; leave 4″ of binding extending from end to make hanging loop. Slip-stitch sides of extended seam binding together, fold, and stitch end to back binding of pot holder.

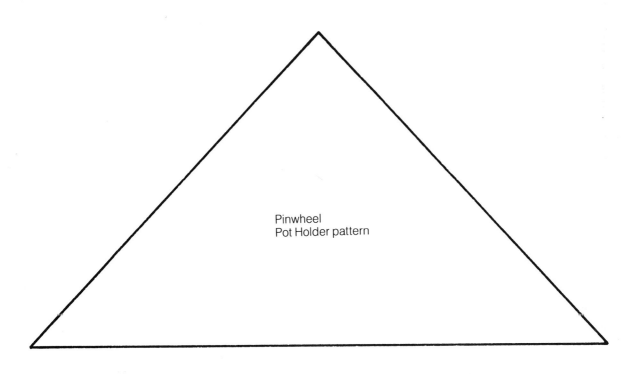

Pinwheel
Pot Holder pattern

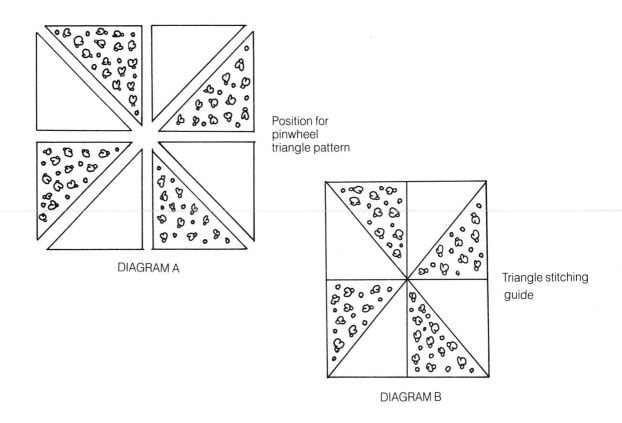

Position for
pinwheel
triangle pattern

DIAGRAM A

Triangle stitching
guide

DIAGRAM B

83

◆ LILY-FLOWER POT HOLDER ◆

◆ *The bold design of the Lily-Flower is offset by a miniature floral pattern used as background fabric. Fast and easy, this oversize pot holder is a good way to practice your patchwork and quilting skills.*

When you've mastered the basic block construction, Lily-Flower blocks can be produced in multiples and used to create table runners, pillows, place mats, or crib quilts.

SIZE: 8½″ × 8½″

MATERIALS *Cotton fabrics:*
- *11″ × 14″ piece blue*
- *1½″ × 4″ piece green*
- *11″ × 22″ piece white print*
- *1¼ yards single-fold bias tape or 1″-wide bias strip*
- *Two 11″ × 11″ squares quilt batting*
- *Blue sewing thread*
- *White quilting thread*

See Enlarging Patterns, page 16. Enlarge A, B, and C pattern pieces. Cut from paper.

From blue fabric cut four A pieces. From white print fabric cut one B piece, two C pieces, one 4″ × 4″ square and one 11″ × 11″ square.

All seams are ¼″. With right sides together, stitch A pieces together according to Diagram A. Press seams open. With right sides together hand-base, then machine-stitch the B piece, C pieces, and 4″ square to A pieces. See Diagram B. Press seams open.

Press long sides and one short side of green fabric piece under ¼″. Center and slip-stitch to B piece to make the Lily-Flower stem. Trim excess fabric at point. Sandwich two layers of quilt batting between top piece and 11″ × 11″ square. Baste layers together.

Quilt pot holder ¼″ from all seams and ½″ from outside edge. Machine-zigzag along outside edge of top piece. Trim excess batting and fabric. Curve corners slightly, taking care not to cut through quilt stitching.

See Binding Edges, page 20. Starting on one corner, seam-bind around pot holder; leave 4″ of binding extending from end to make hanging loop. Slip-stitch sides of extended seam binding together, then fold and stitch end to back binding of pot holder.

Each sq. = 1 in.

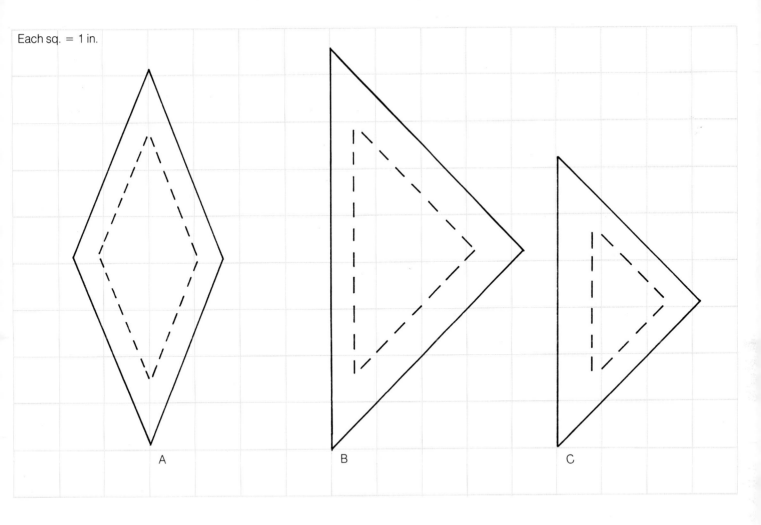

A

B

C

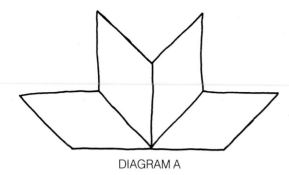

DIAGRAM A

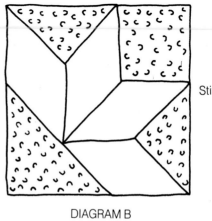

Stitching guide

DIAGRAM B

◆ TRAPUNTO DUCKLING COOKIE JAR ◆

◆ *The "cookie jar" is a gallon-size glass jar, covered with a removable case. The quilting technique is trapunto quilting, which is used to create the puffy, raised duckling appliquéd to the background fabric.*

It's simpler than it sounds. First the *underside of the appliqué is stuffed and the background is then machine-quilted for speedy construction.*

Trapunto Duckling Cookie Jar will keep your freshly baked chocolate-chip cookies full of flavor and give your kitchen an added lift as well.

SIZE: One-gallon glass jar
The pattern requirements for this project apply to a one-gallon jar, but any jar can be covered using the following measurements. For the A pattern, make a rectangle by measuring the circumference of the jar, plus 2″ by the height of the jar plus ½″. The B pattern is a rectangle of the same length as A by 5″ high. To make C, trace around the bottom of the jar and add ½″ all around.

MATERIALS *Cotton fabrics:*
  16″ × 23″ and 7″ × 7″ pieces print
  12″ × 24″ and 7″ × 7″ pieces muslin or any lightweight backing fabric
  4″ × 5″ piece yellow
  12″ × 24″ piece quilt batting
  Small handful polyester stuffing
  11″ piece ¼″-wide elastic
  1 yard ½″-wide satin ribbon

See Enlarging Patterns, page 16. Enlarge pattern pieces and cut from paper. Letter each pattern according to diagram. From print fabric cut one A, B, and C piece. Cut one C piece from 7″ × 7″ piece of backing fabric and one duckling from yellow fabric. On A piece, mark diagonal quilting lines 1″ apart. Measuring 3½″ from bottom edge, center and pin duckling into place on A. Slip-stitch duckling into place, turning edges under ⅛″ as you sew and leaving 1″ opening along bottom edge. Fill duckling with polyester stuffing, using knitting needle to push stuffing into opening. Slip-stitch opening closed.

Sandwich quilt batting between A piece and backing fabric. Working from center outward, baste layers together. By machine, contour-quilt around duckling ⅛″ beyond edge. Machine-stitch over diagonal quilting lines, starting from center and working outward. Machine-zigzag along each edge of A. Trim excess batting and backing fabric.

Press long sides of B under ¼″. Lining up folded edges, press B in half lengthwise. Pin, then machine-stitch B to top of A by placing A piece ¼″ inside folded opening of B and topstitching ⅛″ from edge.

Make casing for elastic by stitching two parallel lines ⅜″ apart across B. Stitch first line ¼″ from bottom edge. Insert safety pin through one end of elastic and push it through casing. Secure each end of elastic with a few stitches. Stitch side seam of A and B closed with ¼″ seam allowance.

Topstitch C pieces together ⅛″ from edge. Gathering bottom edge of A slightly, pin, and then machine-stitch C into place on bottom of A with ¼″ seam allowance.

Slip jar cover onto jar and tie a bow around neck with satin ribbon.

Each sq. = 1 in.

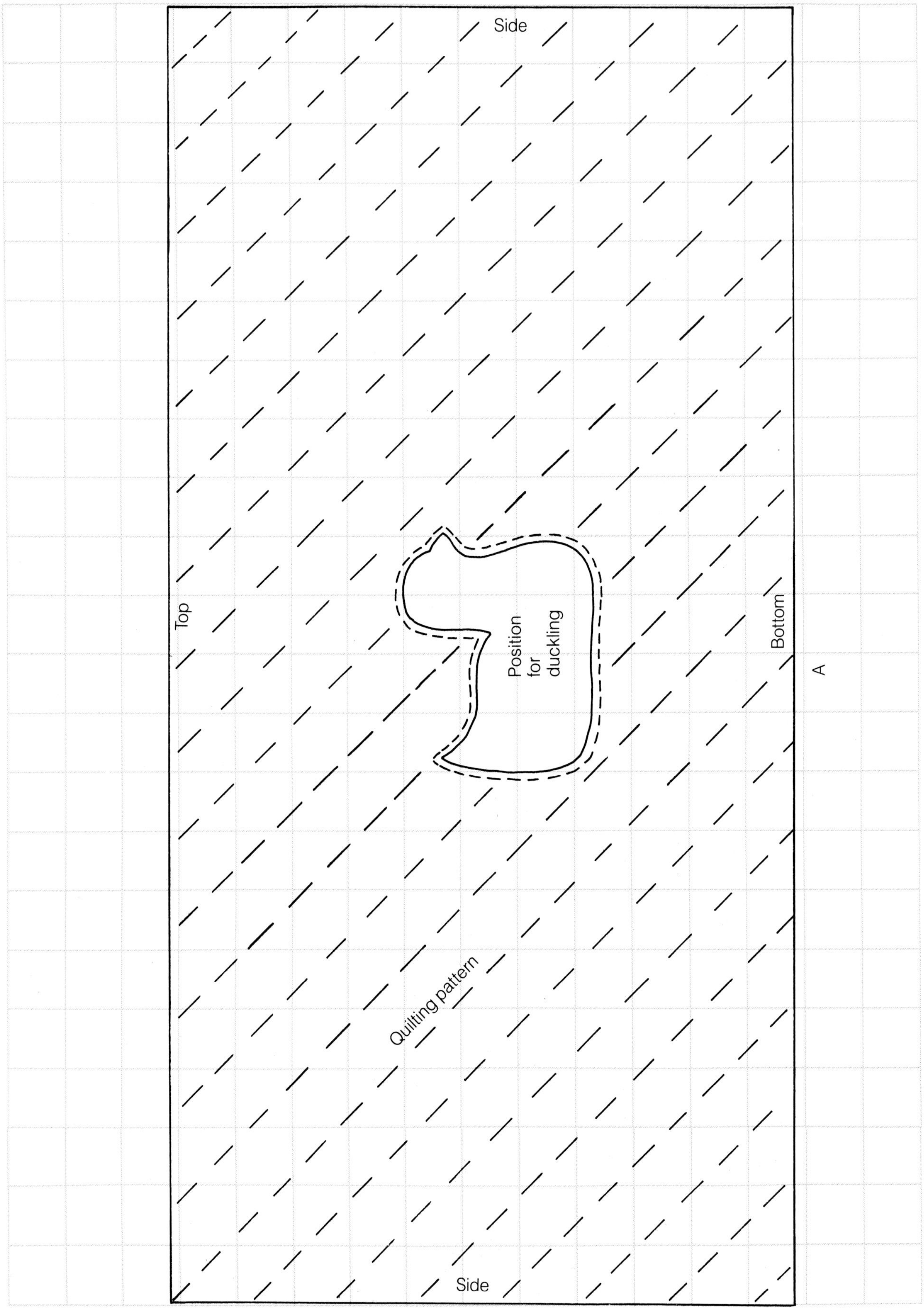

Side

Top

Position
for
duckling

Bottom

A

Quilting pattern

Side

Each sq. = 1 in.

Side

Fold line

B

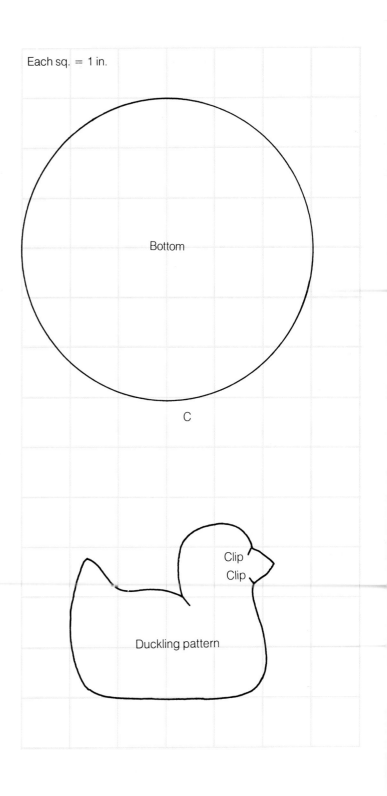

Each sq. = 1 in.

Bottom

C

Clip

Clip

Duckling pattern

◆ FAVORITE FELINE BUN WARMER ◆

◆ *This bun warmer is a sweet kitty cat designed to keep your biscuits, rolls, and cornbread toasty-warm. And it's perfect for Sunday brunch or late-night supper. The "cat" motif is defined by an embroidered backstitch, which also creates a* *fluffy, quilted effect. It's great fun to make—for yourself or as a gift.*

For a real cat lover, stitch up a matching Favorite Feline pillow simply by stuffing the bun warmer and sewing the bottom edge closed.

SIZE: 9″ × 14½″

MATERIALS

¾ *yard cotton fabric*

Two 10″ × 16″ pieces extra-loft quilt batting

6-strand embroidery floss: 1 yard each of red and green, and 1 skein of black

1 yard single-fold bias tape

White quilting thread

Sewing thread to match fabric

See Enlarging Patterns, page 16. Enlarge cat pattern and cut from paper. Draw facial features.

Draw stitching guide (broken lines) on cat pattern. With cotton fabric folded double, trace and cut out two cat pieces. Place one cutout cat piece right side down on dressmaker's carbon paper. Place cat pattern on fabric and trace over stitching guide with a sharp pencil.

See Embroidery Stitches, page 22. Using embroidery floss and backstitch, outline the eyes with black and the mouth with red. Using satin stitch, fill in the nose with red, the pupils with black, and the eyes with green.

Sandwich piece of quilt batting between embroidered cat front and a 10″ × 16″ piece of cotton fabric. Baste the layers together. Using a backstitch, quilt over stitching lines with black embroidery floss.

Sandwich a piece of quilt batting between remaining cat piece and the other 10″ × 16″ piece of cotton fabric. Baste layers together. Following stitching guide on Diagram A, quilt with white quilting thread. Outside stitching line is 1″ from edge, and vertical stitching lines are 1″ apart. Baste around outside edge of cat front and back pieces with ⅛″ seam. Trim away excess quilt batting and fabric.

See Binding Edges, page 20.

From notch to notch, bind bottom of both cat pieces. With right sides together, machine-stitch unbound top portion of cat pieces together, using a ¼″ seam allowance. Turn stitched cat right side out.

Each sq. = 1 in.

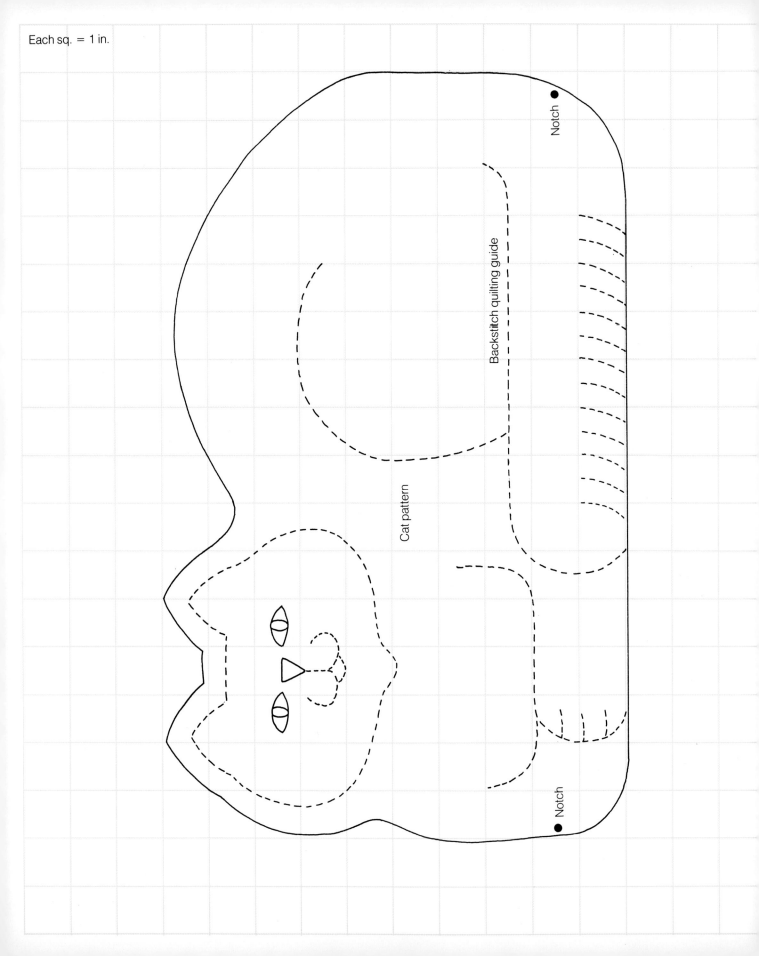

Notch

Backstitch quilting guide

Cat pattern

Notch

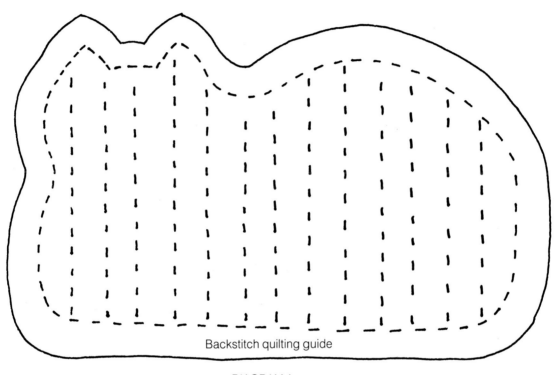

Backstitch quilting guide

DIAGRAM A

KEEPERS AND CARRIERS

◆ BLUE THISTLE SEWING BASKET ◆

◆ *Here's the sewing basket you've always wanted. Instead of the traditional patchwork or appliqué, embroidery is used to create the thistle motif.*

Contour quilting accents the Blue Thistle, and the blue and green of the thistles is repeated in the delicate flower border.

Your Blue Thistle Sewing Basket will *make the perfect storage bin for sewing supplies. And it's such a cheery, decorative item that it's bound to brighten the dullest room. It's a welcome gift for the experienced seamstress as well as the novice. Fill your basket with a bright yellow tape measure, a card of pearl buttons, lace seam binding....*

SIZE: Round basket with lid 9" in diameter

MATERIALS

9" × 18" piece lightweight white cotton fabric

9" × 9" piece quilt batting

1¼ yards ⅞"-wide embroidered trim

6-strand embroidery floss: 3½ yards each of blue and green

White sewing thread

White glue

Round basket with lid 9" in diameter

White quilting thread

See Enlarging Patterns, page, 16. Enlarge embroidery pattern on paper.

Divide 9" × 18" piece of fabric into two 9" × 9" squares. With a compass, draw 8" circle onto one square; draw a second 5½" circle centered inside 8" circle. Place embroidery pattern under fabric, centered inside 5½" circle. Trace embroidery pattern directly onto fabric.

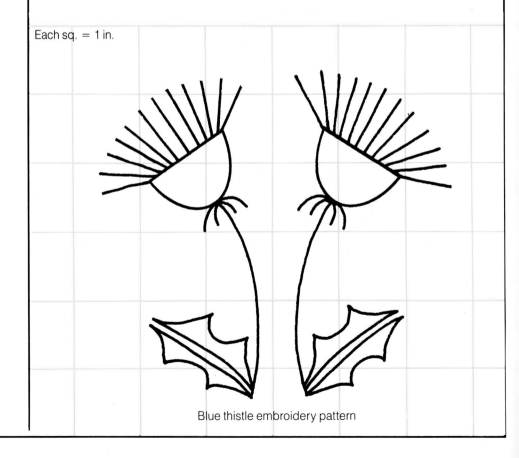

Each sq. = 1 in.

Blue thistle embroidery pattern

See Embroidery Stitches, page 22. Using green floss and satin stitch, fill in leaves. Embroider stems with green floss and stem stitch. Using blue floss and satin stitch, fill in bottom portion of thistles. Embroider thistle petals with blue floss and stem stitch.

Sandwich quilt batting between 9" × 9" fabric squares. Baste layers together. Contour-quilt ¼" from outside edge of embroidered thistle motif. Quilt a second row of stitches ¼" away from the first. With three strands of blue floss, quilt over traced 5½" circle.

Machine-zigzag over traced 8" circle. Trim excess fabric and batting. Using double strand of thread, hand-stitch a running stitch ¼" from raw edge of fabric. Place circle on basket lid. Pull thread ends to gather the fabric until it fits snugly on the lid. Tie thread ends.

Cut 20" piece of trim. Lining up bottom edge of trim with raw edge of fabric, pin trim into place around edge of lid with top of trim at top rim of lid (see photograph). Carefully remove fabric from lid, keeping trim in place. Machine-stitch trim to fabric along top edge of trim.

Glue stitched fabric circle to basket lid. Glue remaining trim around bottom edge of basket.

◆ *This is a fine project for beginners. It can even be made from scrap fabrics, and the results are always pleasing. An* attractive case for needles of all kinds, Hideaway Needle Case would make a thoughtful gift.

SIZE: 3½" × 4"

MATERIALS

11½" × 13" piece cotton print fabric
5" × 11½" piece quilt batting
6½" piece ¾"-wide trim
White quilting thread
Sewing thread to match fabric
Size No. 2 snap

Trace pattern pieces and cut from paper. Following pattern diagram, draw quilting lines on A pattern.

Cut two A pieces from fabric. Place one A piece right side down on dressmaker's carbon paper. Place pattern on top of fabric and trace over quilting lines with a pencil. Pin A pieces right sides together with quilt batting underneath. Machine-stitch together, with a ¼" seam; leave 2½" opening along one narrow end for turning. Trim excess quilt batting and corners. Turn needle case right side out.

Cut 3" piece of trim and fold it in half to make loop. Center and pin loop in 2½" opening. Slip-stitch opening closed, catching trim as you sew. Measuring ⅛" from edge, baste around perimeter of A. With trim loop on your right, follow traced lines and start quilting needle case from center outward. To make the pocket, cut one B piece from fabric. Press top edge under ¼" and machine-hem. Machine-stitch remaining 3½" piece of trim across top of B. Press pocket edges under ¼". Pin, then slipstitch pocket to inside center panel of needle case.

Center and sew a snap to first inside panel of needle case, ¼" away from trim loop. Fold needle case to closed position and with a pencil, mark a dot where the snap meets fabric. Sew the remaining side of snap into place on dot.

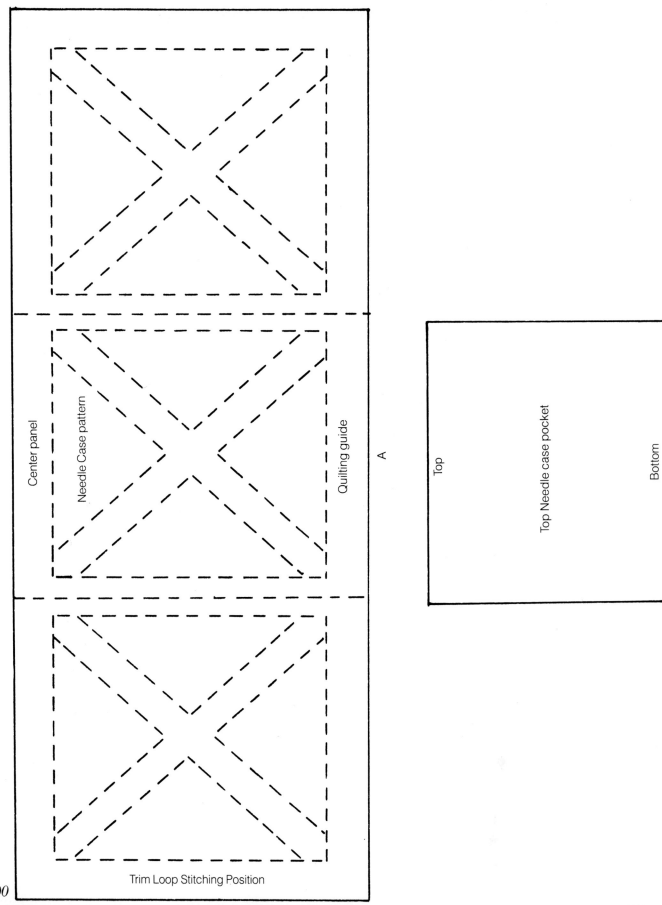

Center panel

Needle Case pattern

Quilting guide

Trim Loop Stitching Position

A

Top

Top Needle case pocket

Bottom

100

◆ BUTTERFLY PINCUSHION ◆

◆ *This charming, stuffed pincushion is appliquéd and quilted, then embellished with tiny faux pearls. Attach a loop and you can hang it on a wall or bulletin board above a sewing table, or string it from your belt when you're pinning fabric. Elegant and fun, it will be a beautiful addition to your sewing room.*

SIZE: *6″ × 6″*

MATERIALS *Cotton fabrics:*

Two 8″ × 8″ pieces print

3″ × 5½″ piece print for wing appliqué

1½″ × 3″ piece print for body appliqué

8″ × 8″ piece muslin or any lightweight backing fabric

8″ × 8″ piece quilt batting

10″ piece ½″-wide ribbon: picot edge, satin, velvet, or other material

Twenty-six 4mm simulated pearls

Few handfuls polyester stuffing

Quilting thread

Sewing thread to match fabrics

Trace and cut pattern pieces from paper. Trace butterfly pattern onto right side of one 8″ × 8″ piece of print fabric.

Trace and cut out wing appliqué from 3″ × 5½″ piece of fabric. Cut body appliqué from 1½″ × 3″ piece of fabric. Following pattern diagram pin, then slip-stitch wing appliqué into place on traced butterfly, turning the edges under ⅛″ with your thumb and forefinger as you sew. Stitch body appliqué into place in the same manner.

Sandwich batting between backing fabric and appliquéd butterfly top piece. Baste the layers together and quilt, following pattern diagram (broken lines). Quilt ⅛″ inside wing appliqué. Zigzag stitch along inside edge of traced butterfly line. Trim excess fabric and batting. Fold ribbon in half. Lining up raw edges, baste ribbon to right side of butterfly at center top. See Diagram A.

With right sides together, pin remaining 8″ × 8″ piece of print fabric to quilted butterfly piece. Machine-stitch with ¼″ seam, leaving a 2″ opening along top of one wing. Trim the excess fabric, clip curves, and turn right side out. Fill with polyester stuffing and slip-stitch opening closed.

Starting at top edge of body appliqué, stitch thirteen pearls ¾″ apart and ⅛″ from outside edge of each wing. Stitch pearls with a continuous strand of double thread.

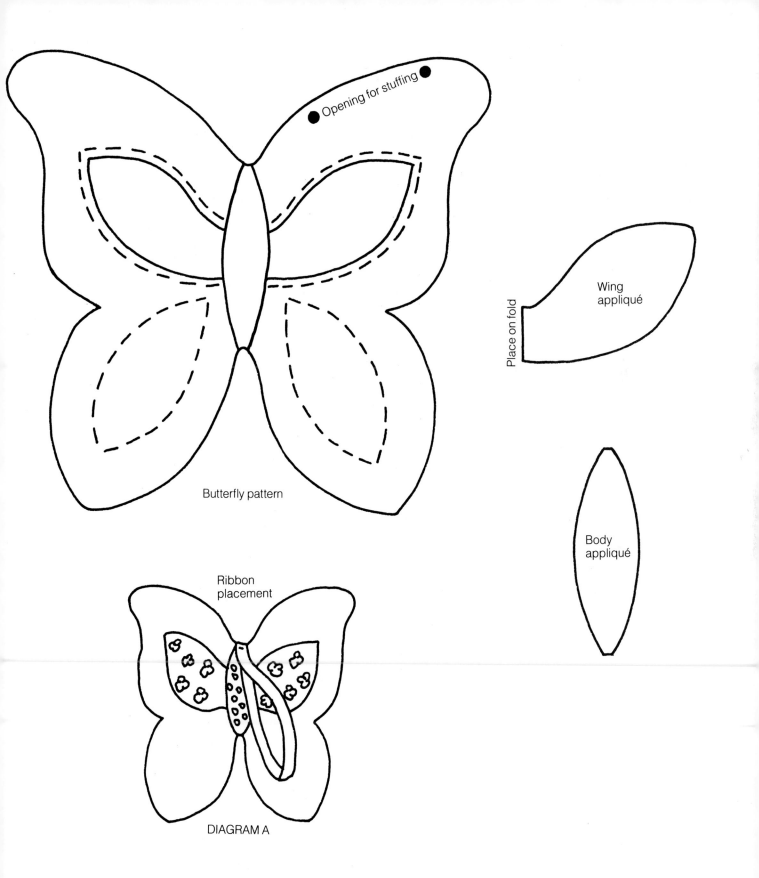

Opening for stuffing

Butterfly pattern

Place on fold

Wing
appliqué

Body
appliqué

Ribbon
placement

DIAGRAM A

◆ SAFEKEEPING SCISSORS CASE ◆

◆ *This is just the thing to keep scissors handy, or perhaps you'd prefer to use it for carry-along projects. It's appliquéd and quilted, and can be made to fit scissors of any size.*

Easy to make, Safe-keeping Scissors Case is a great gift for anyone who loves creative stitchery.

SIZE: 4″ × 7½″

MATERIALS *Cotton fabrics:*

12″ × 24″ piece muslin, cut into four 6″ × 12″ sections

4″ × 8″ piece dark print

3″ × 6″ piece pastel print

2″ × 3½″ piece pastel print

1″ × 28″ piece dark print cut on bias to be used as seam binding

Two 6″ × 12″ pieces quilt batting

White quilting thread

Sewing thread to match fabrics

Size No. 3 snap

See Enlarging Patterns, page 16. Enlarge A, B, C, and D pattern pieces. Cut from paper. Letter each piece according to diagrams.

Fold A pattern on fold line and again down center. Open A and pin to piece of muslin. Outline pattern with a sharp pencil. Make placement markings on muslin (outside of outline) by making a dot at the end of each fold line. Fold A pattern on fold line to make A¹, using bottom portion only. Outline A¹ on another piece of muslin. Do not cut out A or A¹.

Outline and cut out B from dark print, and C and D from pastel print pieces. Press edges under ¼″. Center B on A, lining up four corners of B with placement markings on A. Pin or baste into place, then sew using a slip-stitch. Repeat this procedure with C and D.

Sandwich a piece of quilt batting between appliquéd A top piece and another piece of muslin. Baste all three layers together and quilt, following stitching guide (broken lines) marked on pattern diagram. Make another quilt sandwich with A¹ and quilt, following stitching guide below fold line. Fill in center area with quilt lines ¼″ apart and parallel to outer quilt lines.

Cut out quilted A and A¹ carefully, following penciled outline. Bind top raw edge of A¹ with 5″ bias-fabric strip. Trim away excess on each side. See Binding Edges, page 20. With right sides out and basting together 1″ from raw edges, place A on A¹. With remaining bias-fabric strip, bind around entire perimeter of scissors case; use ¼″ seam allowance and attach A¹ to A as you sew.

Center and sew snap on inside of flap ¼″ from top. Fold flap down and mark a dot with pencil where the center of snap falls on A¹. Sew remaining side of snap into place on dot.

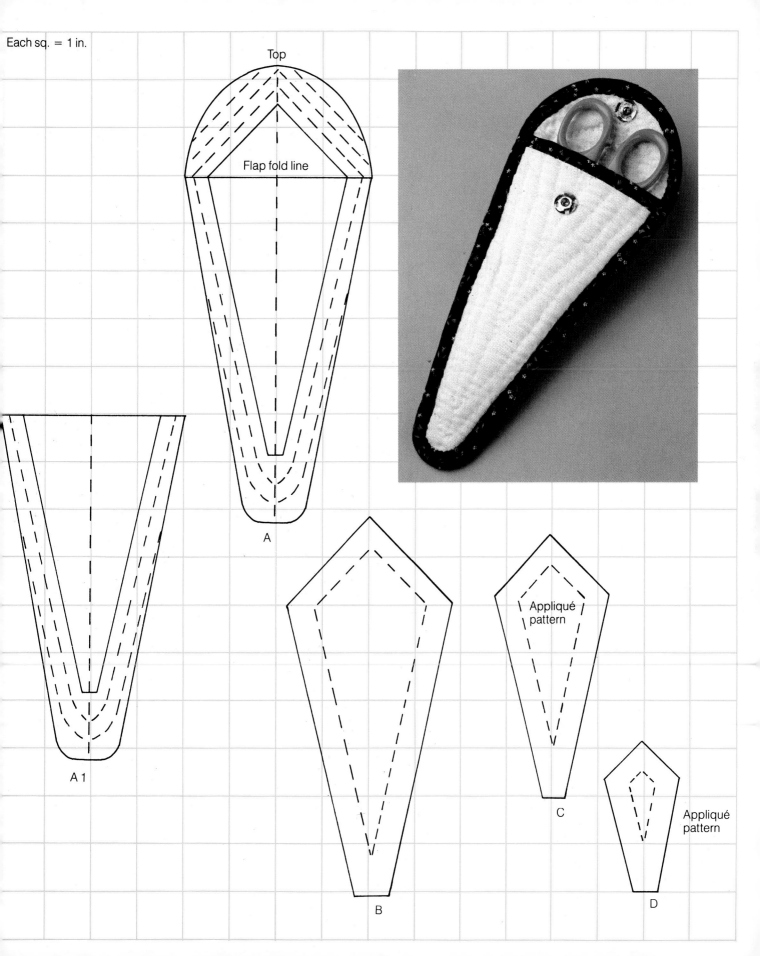

Each sq. = 1 in.

Top

Flap fold line

A

A 1

B

C

Appliqué pattern

D

Appliqué pattern

◆ ORIENTAL FOLDER ◆

◆ *This is a very special quilted desk accessory. You can fill it with love letters, scented writing paper, or business documents. It is designed to hold papers measuring 8½″ × 11″.*

The Oriental pattern of the blue fabric *blends beautifully with the creamy-white print fabric in the background. The edges are bound with strips of bias binding, and the flap is held closed with a satiny frog closure. Oriental Folder would make an attractive birthday or graduation gift.*

SIZE: 10″ × 12″

MATERIALS *Cotton fabrics:*
⅜ yard 45″-wide off-white print
⅜″ yard 45″-wide blue print
Two 11½″ × 12½″ pieces and one 11½″ × 7″ piece extra-loft quilt batting
Frog closure
Quilting thread
Sewing thread to match fabrics

See Enlarging Patterns, page 16. Enlarge triangle pattern. Cut from paper.

From blue print fabric, mark and cut five triangles and five 1″ × 13″ bias strips. Press short sides of three triangles under ¼″. Following pattern diagram, mark quilting lines on triangle pieces (broken lines).

From off-white print, cut four 11″ × 12″ rectangles. Lining up raw edges pin, then slip-stitch two turned-under triangles to right side of one rectangle. Pin remaining turned-under triangle to right side of another rectangle. See Diagram A.

To make quilting easier, trim background fabric away from beneath triangle appliqués ½″ from seams. Following Diagram B, mark contour quilting lines on background fabric ¼″ from appliqués and at 1″ intervals. On unappliquéd top portion of front rectangle, mark quilting lines according to triangle pattern diagram.

Sandwich quilt batting between appliquéd and unappliquéd rectangles. Carefully lining up raw edges, baste layers together. Quilt over marked lines.

Make flap by lining up raw edges and sandwiching top 11″ side of folder back between remaining two triangles. Machine-stitch with ¼″ seam. Fold triangles away from rectangle. See Diagram C.

Sandwich batting between triangles, making sure batting is against seam. Baste layers together, then quilt over marked lines. Machine-zigzag along outside edges of folder front and back pieces.

See Binding Edges, page 20. With one bias strip, bind top edge of front folder. Stitch remaining bias strips together to form one long strip. Press seams open.

With wrong sides together, pin folder front to folder back. Starting at tip of flap bind around entire folder with ¼″ seam, stitching folder front to folder back as you sew. Fold flap down and stitch frog closure to front of the folder.

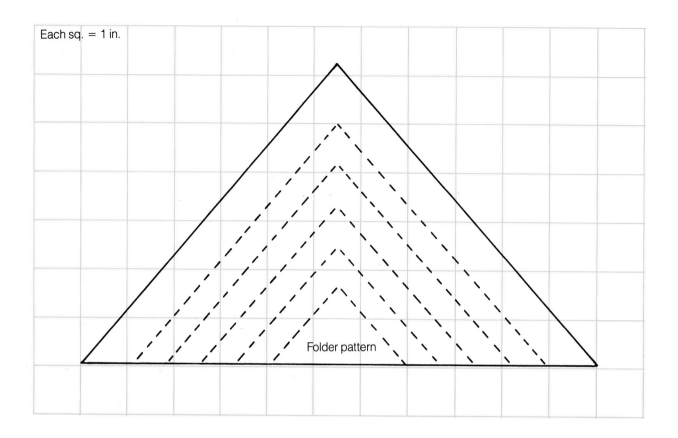

Each sq. = 1 in.

Folder pattern

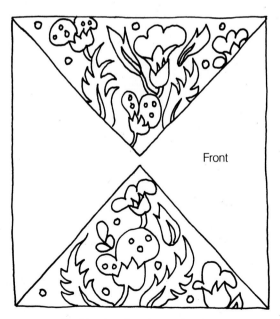

Front

Position for triangle appliqué

Back

DIAGRAM A

108

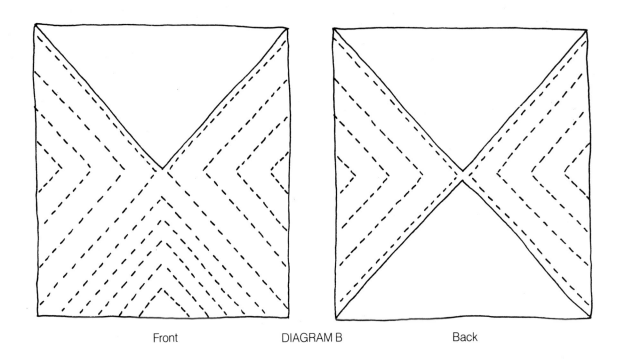

Front   DIAGRAM B   Back

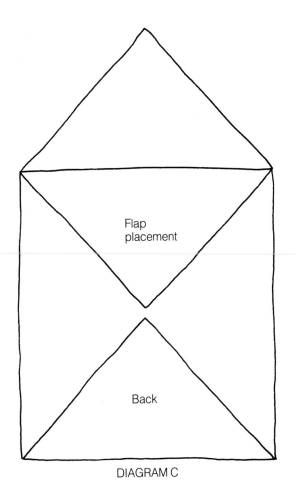

Flap
placement

Back

DIAGRAM C

◆ CUPID'S QUIVER SACHET POCKET ◆

◆ *This scented heart, with its pastel floral pattern and lacy edging, brings back memories of a bygone era. A potpourri or lavender sachet placed in the quilted front pocket will lend its delicate fragrance to a room, closet, or drawer. Or fill the pocket with dried flowers and hang it on a wall. However you choose to use it, this sachet is a romantic and portable way to freshen the air with aromatic herbs and flowers.*

SIZE: 10″ × 10″

MATERIALS

¼ yard pink print, polished cotton fabric

1 yard 1¼″-wide gathered pink eyelet lace

1 yard 1½″-wide dark-pink gathered lace

1¼ yards ¼″-wide satin ribbon

6½″ × 9½″ piece quilt batting

4 oz. polyester stuffing

Sewing thread to match fabric

White quilting thread

See Enlarging Patterns, page 16. Enlarge heart pattern and draw quilting guide (broken lines). Cut pattern from paper.

From fabric cut one heart piece and one 9″ × 10″ rectangle. To make pocket, fold heart pattern on fold line. Using bottom portion as pattern, cut two pocket pieces. Place one pocket piece right side down on dressmaker's carbon paper. Place pattern on top of fabric and trace over quilting lines with a sharp pencil.

Place pocket pieces right sides together with batting under fabric. Machine-stitch across top straight edge with ¼″ seam. Turn pocket pieces right sides out, with batting sandwiched between fabric. Baste layers together, then quilt over marked lines. Trim excess batting. Lining up raw edges, baste quilted pocket to right side of heart piece with ⅛″ seam.

Cut 12″ piece of satin ribbon. Fold in half to make hanging loop. Lining up raw edges, baste ribbon to center top V of heart. Lining up the raw edge of the heart piece with the top (gathered) edge of eyelet lace, machine-baste lace to right side heart piece, starting at center top V of heart and using ¼″ seam. Lining up top edges, baste gathered lace directly on top of eyelet lace.

With right sides together, machine-stitch heart to 9″ × 10″ fabric rectangle with ⅜″ seam. Leave 4″ opening along one side for stuffing. Trim the excess fabric.

Turn right side out and stuff. Slip-stitch opening closed.

Tie remaining satin ribbon into a bow and stitch to center top heart at V. Fill pocket with your favorite potpourri or sachet.

Each sq. = 1 in.

Pocket fold line

Quilting guide

Heart and heart pocket pattern

◆ ANGEL-WING IRIS EYEGLASS CASE ◆

◆ *This is an easy-to-make bazaar best-seller or a self-styled treat for yourself.*

Angel-Wing Iris Eyeglass Case is a smart and stylish way to protect your eyeglasses.

SIZE: 4½" × 6½"

MATERIALS *Cotton fabrics:*
7½" × 20" piece off-white
5" × 7" piece purple
1½" × 2" piece yellow
30" piece single-fold bias tape or 1"-wide bias strip
Two 5½" × 7½" pieces quilting batting
Thread to match yellow and purple fabrics
White quilting thread

Trace A, B, C, and D pattern pieces. Cut from paper.

From purple fabric, cut two A and B pieces and one C piece. From yellow fabric, cut one D piece. From off-white fabric, cut two 4½" × 7" rectangles.

Following Diagram A, slip-stitch A, B, C, and D appliqués into place on one 4½" × 7" rectangle, turning the edges under ⅛" as you sew. Draw diagonal quilting lines ½" apart on remaining rectangle.

From off-white fabric, cut two 5" × 7½" rectangles to make lining for eyeglass case. Sandwich quilt batting between 4½" × 7" rectangles and lining rectangles. Baste layers together.

Quilt ¼" inside appliqué edges. Contour-quilt around iris ⅛" outside appliqué edge. Continue contour-quilting at ¼" intervals until entire rectangle is quilted.

Quilt over drawn lines on back piece of eyeglass case. Machine-zigzag along outside edges of 4½" × 7" rectangles. Trim excess batting and fabric.

See Binding Edges, page 20. All seams are ¼". Bind the top edge of front and back pieces of eyeglass case. With wrong sides together, machine-baste case front to back; leave top edge open. Curve bottom corners slightly. Bind sides and bottom of eyeglass case.

URING the Season, dance⟨⟩ were given almost every nigh⟨⟩ Sunday. The most exciting were⟨⟩ such as the ones given twice a ye⟨⟩ and Princess of Wales and som⟨⟩ possessors of houses with la⟨⟩s, all ages and ranks of the ⟨⟩ here that a successful y⟨⟩ced to an appropriate⟨⟩ Married women ⟨⟩, and often cou⟨⟩ married daughter⟨⟩ often preferred the ol⟨⟩nger one's still-shy sch⟨⟩s frequently in the country⟨⟩ls, squire's balls and others ⟨⟩ nities to keep their steps polis⟨⟩s were the Quadrille, the Lancer ⟨⟩ Quadrille and the Lancer's were bo⟨⟩s of complicated steps that the dance⟨⟩s energetic and in polite society the ⟨⟩l but not boisterous. The waltz was the ⟨⟩dered to be much superior to the ⟨⟩ Albert up late dancing it; the guests at ⟨⟩oming-of-age party danced it until ⟨⟩urchill went into premature labor ⟨⟩re prime minister, while waltzing ⟨⟩e dancers refreshed a light (by ⟨⟩ supper was served – champagne, ⟨⟩en salad, cakes, jellies, ices, ⟨⟩d small hams – after which the ⟨⟩:00 in the morning.

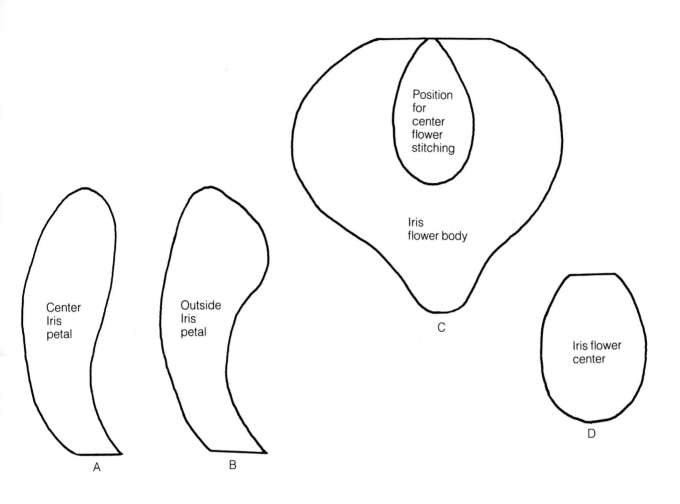

Center
Iris
petal

A

Outside
Iris
petal

B

Position
for
center
flower
stitching

Iris
flower body

C

Iris flower
center

D

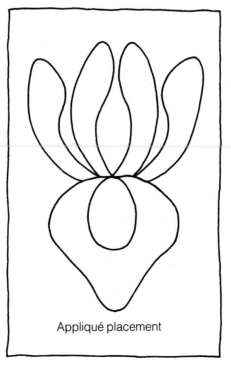

Appliqué placement

DIAGRAM A

◆ SUN-BLOSSOM BELT ◆

◆ *Here's a versatile accessory that can be made in a variety of color combinations. The belt will give new summer whites a smart look and brighten last year's out-* *fits, too. An interchangeable accessory with plenty of design strength, this attractive belt is easily adapted to today's changing fashions.*

SIZE: 3½" wide

MATERIALS *Cotton fabrics:*
  ⅜ yard 45"-wide light purple
  3½" × 7" piece dark purple
  6" × 8" piece orange
  5" × 36" (approximately) size depends on waist measurement
Two heavy-duty waistband hooks and eyes
Sewing thread to match fabrics
White quilting thread

See Enlarging Patterns, page 16. Enlarge and cut A and B patterns from paper.

To make belt pattern, enlarge and draw pattern on paper. Do not cut out. Measure waist and add 4" to this measurement. Enlarged belt pattern is 14" in length; subtract 14" from waist measurement. Divide this number by 2. Add the divided total to each side of belt pattern. Example: For 28" waist, waist measurement plus 4" equals 32". 14" subtracted from 32" equals 18"; 18" divided by two equals 9". Draw 9" extension on each side of belt pattern. Length for belt pattern equals 32".

Draw quilting guide (broken lines) on belt pattern, extending lines to end of pattern. Cut out pattern. Place dressmaker's carbon paper right side down on light-purple fabric. Place belt pattern on top of paper and trace around out-side edge of pattern and over quilting lines. Cut out traced belt piece.

From dark-purple fabric, cut one A pattern piece. From orange fabric, cut five B pattern pieces. Center and pin A appliqué to belt piece. Slip-stitch into place, turning edges under ¼" as you sew. Press B appliqué edges under ¼". Arrange on A appliqué in Sun-Blossom motif. Slip-stitch into place.

From light-purple fabric, cut rectangle 5" wide by length of belt plus 1". Place belt piece right side together with rectangle. Pin batting under rectangle. Machine-stitch around outside edge of belt with ¼" seam, leaving 4" opening along bottom edge for turning.

Trim excess batting and fabric. Turn right side out and slip-stitch opening closed. Baste belt layers together, then quilt over marked lines. Stitch hooks and eyes into place at belt ends.

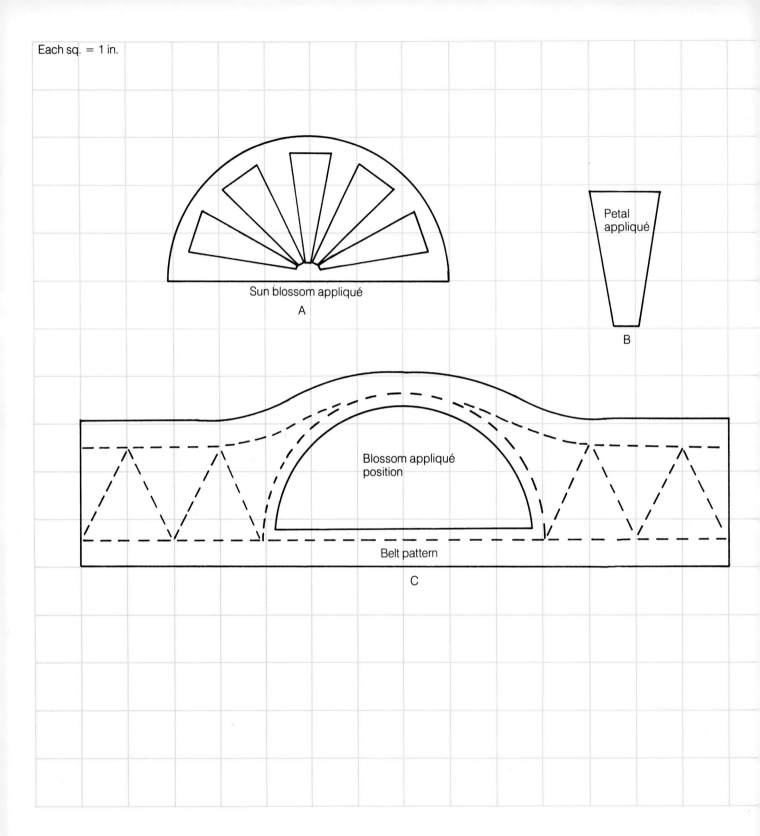

Each sq. = 1 in.

Petal
appliqué

Sun blossom appliqué

A

B

Blossom appliqué
position

Belt pattern

C

◆ CROWN JEWELS TRINKET BOX ◆

◆ *This is a luxurious wooden box with a covered top that is quilted and embellished with small faux pearls. For sumptuous appeal, frilly eyelet lace and satiny upholstery gimp encircle the lid. Your trinket box will become a practical heirloom when you realize that it is a beautiful no-nonsense way of keeping rings, bracelets, earrings, pins, and lockets at your fingertips.*

SIZE: Round wooden box 6″ in diameter

MATERIALS *Cotton fabrics:*
8½″ × 17″ piece pink print
3″ × 4½″ piece yellow print
9″ × 9″ piece muslin or any lightweight backing fabric
Three 9″ × 9″ pieces extra-loft quilt batting
20″ piece ½″-wide upholstery gimp
20″ piece 1-¼″-wide eyelet lace
Approximately sixty 4mm faux pearls
6″ × 6″ piece lightweight cardboard
Quilting thread
Thread to match fabrics
White glue
Round wooden box with lid, 6″ in diameter

Trace crown pattern and cut from paper.

Cut two 8″ circles from pink fabric. Cut one 6″ circle (trace bottom of box) from cardboard and two from batting. Following Diagram A, mark horizontal and vertical quilting lines ¾″ apart on one 8″ fabric circle.

Cut one crown from yellow fabric. Center and slip-stitch crown to marked circle, turning edges under ⅛″ as you sew and leaving a 2″ opening along bottom edge. Using knitting needle or some other pointed object, stuff small scraps of batting into opening. Stitch opening closed.

Quilt crown appliqué ¼″ in from edges. Sandwich 9″ × 9″ square of batting between appliquéd circle and backing fabric. Baste layers together. Quilt over marked lines, stitching a bead to each intersection. Stitch beads only to 1″ from circle perimeter. Zigzag-stitch around outside edge of circle. Trim excess batting and fabric.

Using double thread, hand-stitch a running stitch ¼″ from quilted circle edge. Pull ends of thread, gathering circle until it fits snugly over box lid. Tie ends; remove circle from lid.

Topstitch lace to underside of gimp. Zigzag ends to prevent fraying. Stitch top edge of gimp to gathered circle ½″ from circle edge. Place 6″ batting circle on box lid and gathered circle on top. Glue circle to lip of lid. Place remaining 6″ batting circle on cardboard circle. Place 8″ fabric circle on top and glue edges to back of cardboard. Glue padded circle to inside bottom of box.

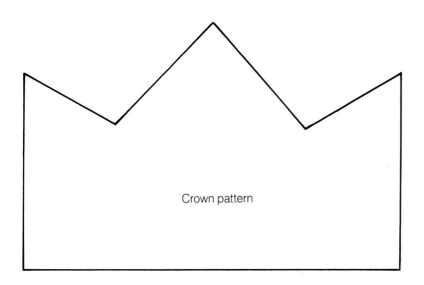

Crown pattern

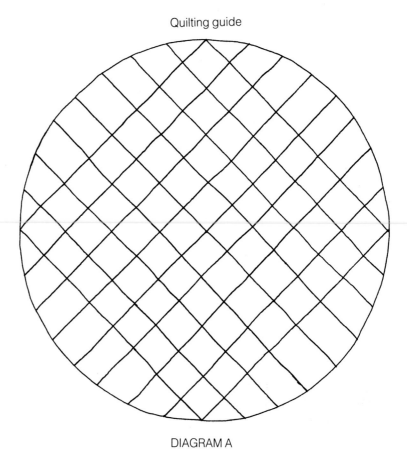

Quilting guide

DIAGRAM A

◆ SPARE POCKET ◆

◆ *Traditional and trendy at the same time, this spare pocket is on the move when you are. It will hold your keys, money, and a small notebook...and* *leaves your hands free for shopping or holding tiny tots. It's appliquéd and quilted, and will snap on and off a store-bought belt. It is a perfect gift.*

SIZE: 6″ × 9″

MATERIALS *Cotton fabrics:*
⅜ yard 45″-wide yellow seersucker
3½″ × 4½″ piece green print
3″ × 3″ piece red
16″ × 16″ square quilt batting
Sewing thread to match fabrics
Three No. 4 snaps
White quilting thread

See Enlarging Patterns, page 16. Enlarge pattern pieces and cut from paper. Fold pattern for pocket back on cutting line to make pocket front.

From yellow fabric cut two pocket backs, two pocket fronts, and two pocket flaps. Following quilting guide (broken lines) on pattern diagram, draw diagonal quilting lines 1″ apart on right side of one pocket front and one flap piece.

From green fabric, cut one stem piece and two leaves. From red fabric, cut one flower piece. Following pattern diagram pin, then slip-stitch appliqué pieces to right side of marked pocket front, turning edges under ⅛″ as you sew.

Adding ½″ all around, cut one pocket back, front, and flap piece from batting. Pin pocket back pieces right sides together, with batting under fabric; pin front pieces, then flap pieces in same manner. With ¼″ seam, machine-stitch around outside edges of each pocket back, front, and flap unit; leave 3½″ opening along bottom edge of back and front. Leave 3½″ opening along top straight edge of flap. Trim excess batting and fabric at corners. Turn pieces right side out. Slip-stitch openings closed.

Baste layers together, then quilt ¼″ inside appliqués on pocket front. Quilt over marked lines on front and flap. Quilt around perimeter of back piece ⅜″ from fabric edge.

With wrong sides together, slip-stitch pocket front to back. Pin, then slip-stitch straight edge of flap ½″ above pocket opening.

To make hanging handle, fold handle to pocket back along fold line. Stitch snap to each corner of handle and pocket back. Stitch snap to center flap front.

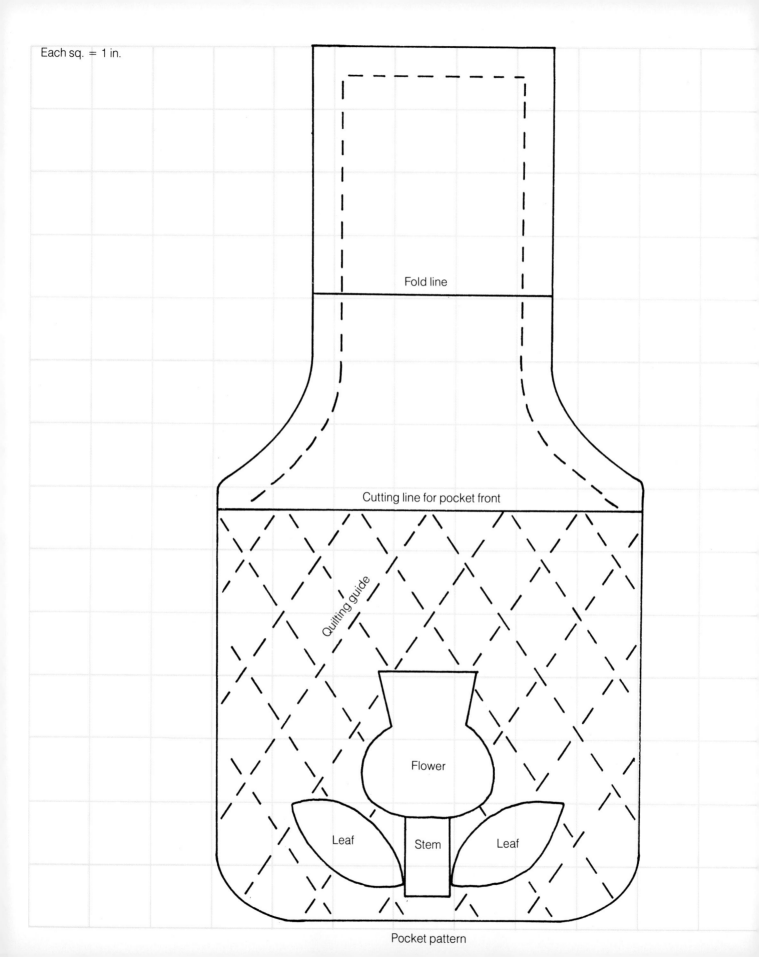

Each sq. = 1 in.

Fold line

Cutting line for pocket front

Quilting guide

Flower

Leaf

Stem

Leaf

Pocket pattern

Each sq. = 1 in.

Top of flap

Pocket flap pattern

Leaf
appliqué

Stem
appliqué

Flower
appliqué

◆ CRAZY LITTLE EVENING BAG ◆

◆ *During the Victorian era, scraps of silk, velvet, and brocade were stitched into elegant crazy quilts and often elaborately decorated with embroidery and beadwork.*

Crazy quilting is a wonderful way to show off needlework skills and use unusual and pretty fabric scraps and remnants at the same time. It's also fairly easy to do. Irregularly shaped fabric scraps are appliquéd, with edges overlapping, to a muslin background. The edges are then embroidered in many different ways.

A bit of whimsy and fashion independence, this romantic evening bag will easily become the extra-special purse to have in your wardrobe.

SIZE: 6½" × 7½"

MATERIALS

8½" × 19½" piece muslin or lightweight cotton backing fabric

8½" × 19½" piece polyester or silk lining

Scraps of velvet, satin, brocade, and other fabrics

6-strand embroidery floss of various colors to contrast fabric scraps

Black No. 4 snap

1 yard bolo cord

Sewing thread to match lining

See Enlarging Patterns, page 16. Enlarge pattern and cut from paper.

For bag back, cut one pattern piece from both muslin and lining. Fold pattern on fold line. Longest side is bag front. From both muslin and lining, cut one bag front.

Starting at raw edge of muslin, pin small pieces of overlapping fabric scraps to bag front and back pieces; turn under raw edges. Fill entire background with fabric. Slip-stitch scrap appliqués into place. Trim excess fabric.

See Embroidery Stitches, page 22. Embroider along outside edges of appliqués with various stitches and colors of floss. Baste straight edge of bag front pieces under ⅜". With right sides together, stitch bag front to back piece and lining front to back piece with ¼" seam. With bag and lining still wrong sides out, line up the basted edges of bag front pieces. Pin, then machine-stitch lining to bag along flap edge. See Diagram A.

Turn flap right side out, press lightly. Turn bag right side out. Insert lining into bag, wrong sides together, and slip-stitch basted edges together. Remove basting. Turn bag wrong side out and tack lining along seam line. Securely stitch ends of bolo cord to seam line on both sides of bag. Turn bag right side out. Center and stitch snap to inside bag front ¼" from straight edge. Finally, stitch the opposite side of the snap to the underside of the flap.

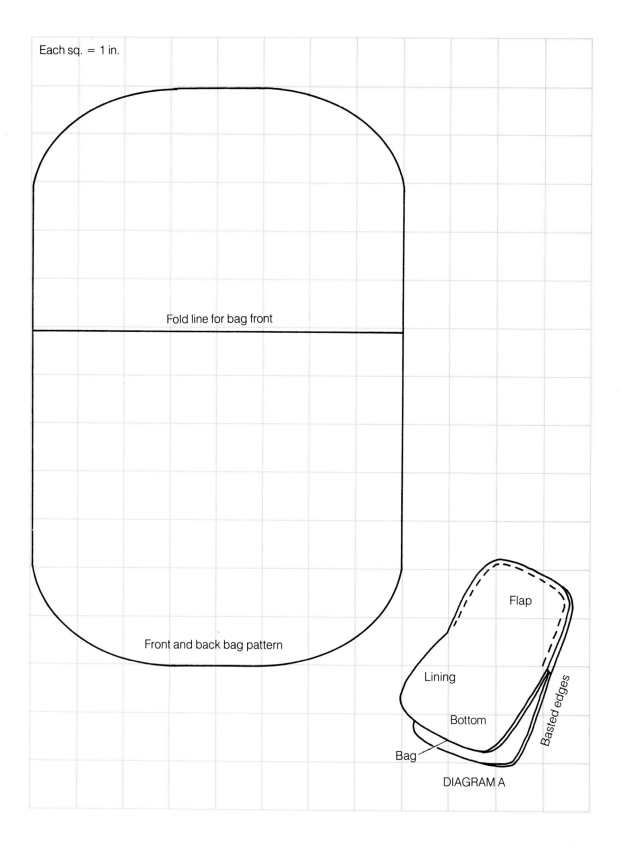

Each sq. = 1 in.

Fold line for bag front

Front and back bag pattern

Flap

Lining

Bottom

Bag

Basted edges

DIAGRAM A

◆ TRIANGULAR LOG-CABIN TOTE ◆

◆ *Although it looks complicated, the log-cabin patchwork motif is among the easiest to make. Fabric "logs" of equal width are stitched around a central fabric block. In this tote the unusual triangular log-cabin design is created by using a fabric triangle at the center.*

You'll love the end result. It has a generous shoulder strap that allows your hands to swing free, and because of the multi-colored design it will miraculously complement your entire wardrobe.

SIZE: 15" × 15"

MATERIALS *Cotton fabrics:*

Two contrasting 8" × 17" pieces solid (orange and blue used here)

1 yard 45"-wide black

Five pieces print fabric in complementary colors, approximately 9" × 13" each

½ yard 36"-wide muslin

Two 16" × 16" squares extra-loft quilt batting

5" × 40" piece fusible interfacing

Sewing thread to match fabrics

Black quilting thread

Trace pattern pieces and cut from paper.

Cut sixteen large triangles from muslin and eight small triangles from both solid fabric pieces. See cutting guide, Diagram A.

Using one print for all sixteen strips of same length, cut sixteen 1"-wide fabric strips in the following lengths. To make fabric selections refer to Diagram B for strip placement: #1—3½", #2—4", #3—6½", #4—5½", #5—6½". For #6 strip, cut eight 10" strips from each solid fabric piece. See Diagram A.

Fold and press each large muslin triangle in half. Open and lay flat. Following Diagram C, center and pin a small triangle to each large triangle. All seams are ¼". With right sides together, stitch fabric strips around outside edge of centered triangle; press each strip back toward outer edge after joining. See Diagram D. Strip #6 is same fabric as center triangle. Press, then trim excess fabric from triangles.

Form eight squares by stitching contrasting triangles together along the #6 strips. Press seams open. Referring to photograph for placement, stitch together two sets of four squares to create front and back panels. From black fabric, mark and cut two 16" × 16" lining squares, four 2½" × 12" border strips, four 2½" × 16" border strips, and one 5" × 40" strap.

Stitch two 12" border strips along opposite sides of each pieced square. Stitch 16" border strips across top and bottom. Press edges of top border strips under ¼".

Press one side of each black square under ¼". Lining up folded edges, sandwich quilt batting between pieced panel and black square. Baste layers together 1" in from outside edge.

Starting ¼" away from seam line of center square, machine-quilt two parallel lines ¼" apart around the square. Trim excess batting. With right sides together, stitch sides and bottom of bag; fold lining fabric back to catch only batting and front panels as you sew. Overlap one side of lining fabric over the (Directions continued page 132.)

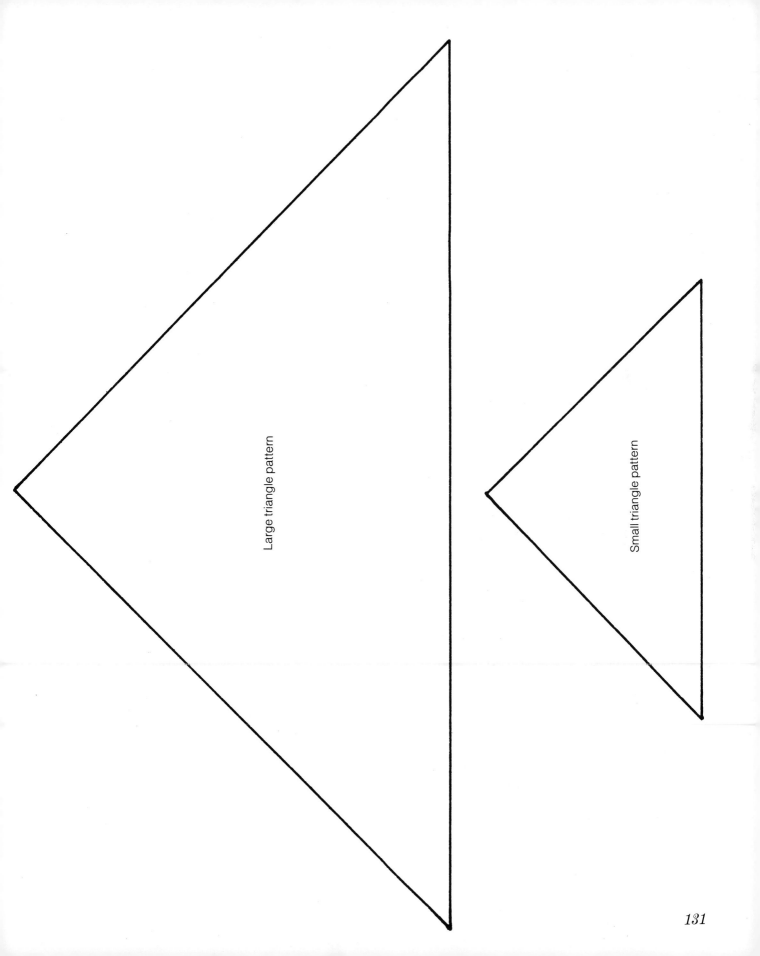

Large triangle pattern

Small triangle pattern

other. Fold overlapped edge under and slip-stitch. Turn bag right side out.

With a hot iron, adhere interfacing to strap. Press both long sides under ¼″. Lining up folded edges, press strap in half lengthwise. Topstitch both sides of strap ⅛″ from the edge. Pin strap ends inside top bag opening. Push any excess batting inside opening and slip-stitch closed, stitching strap securely as you sew.

Cutting guide for 8″ x 17″ solid fabric

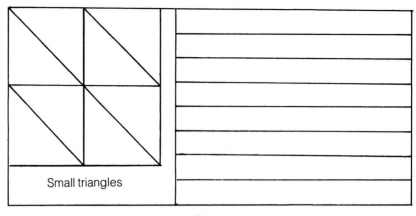

Small triangles

DIAGRAM A

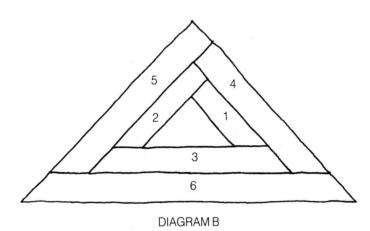

DIAGRAM B

Triangle placement

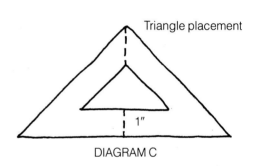

1″

DIAGRAM C

Strip stitching guide

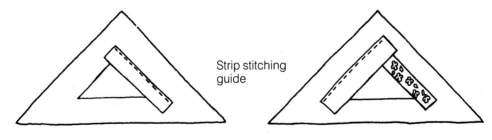

DIAGRAM D

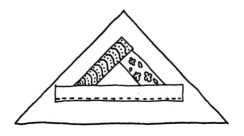

◆ PRETTY-AS-A-PEACOCK COSMETICS BAG ◆

◆ *With this project you'll soon discover that there's no need to work hard to look good. An easy answer to an active life, it allows your cosmetics to travel beautifully and be instantly available when* *you're ready to apply makeup. For added luxury, small glass beads are stitched to the end of each tail feather. And as a practical touch, the bag is quilted to prevent fragile contents from breaking.*

SIZE: 6½″ × 9″

MATERIALS *Cotton fabrics:*
  ¼ yard 45″-wide red print
  4½″ × 6½″ piece blue
  2″ × 3″ piece green
  ¾ yard single-fold bias tape or 1″-wide bias strip
  Two 8″ × 11″ pieces quilt batting
  9″ red zipper
  1 yard black 6-strand embroidery floss
  23 small, round glass beads
  White quilting thread

See Enlarged Pattern, page 16. Enlarge pattern pieces, drawing quilting guide (broken lines) on tail, eyes, and beak of bird and cut from paper.

From red print, cut four 7″ × 9″ rectangles. Press one 9″ side of each rectangle under ¼″. Turning appliqué edges under ¼″ as you sew, center and slip-stitch tail to right side of one rectangle (folded edge on top). Turning appliqué edges under ¼″ as you sew, center and slip-stitch body to tail; leave ¼″ body bottom extending below tail.

Following Diagram A, use simple straight stitches to embroider eyes, beak, head feathers, and feet. Place one side of zipper right side up under folded edge of appliquéd rectangle. Machine-topstitch ¼″ from zipper teeth. Stitch folded edge of another rectangle to unstitched zipper side.

To make bag lining, with wrong sides together, slip-stitch folded edges of remaining rectangles to underside of zipper ¼″ from zip-per teeth. With a pencil, draw curves on bottom corners of right side of outer rectangles. Mark diagonal quilting lines ¾″ apart on right side of bag back. Making sure it is pushed against zipper edge, sandwich batting between lining and outside rectangles. Baste layers together.

Quilt over marked lines on tail appliqué. Contour-quilt around outside edge of peacock ¼″ from appliqué. Continue contour-quilting at ½″ intervals until entire bag front is quilted. Do not quilt past bottom curves. Quilt over drawn lines on bag back. Trim excess fabric and batting at marked curves.

With wrong sides together, stitch bag front to bag back by machine-zigzag stitching along very edge of bag. See Binding Edges, page 20. Bind around outside edge of bag with bias tape. Using double-strand quilting thread, stitch a bead to center top of each tail feather and top of each head feather.

Each sq. = 1 in.

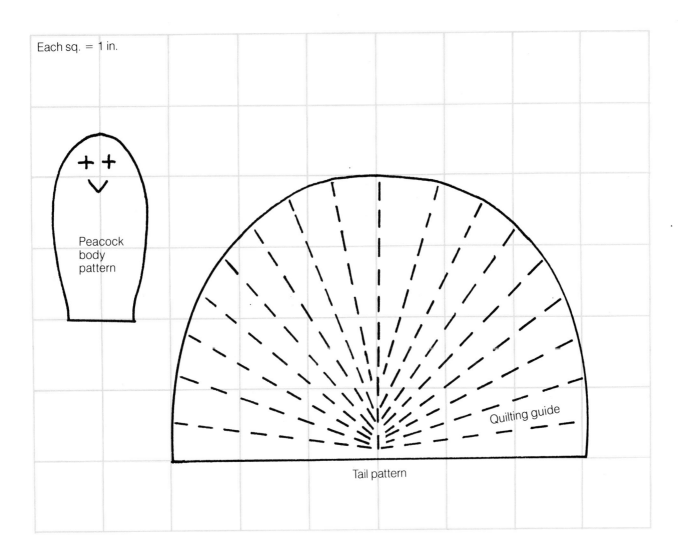

Peacock
body
pattern

Quilting guide

Tail pattern

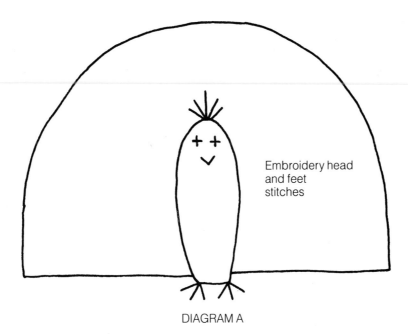

Embroidery head
and feet
stitches

DIAGRAM A

◆ RIBBON JEWELRY ROLL ◆

◆ *Ribbon quilting is the technique used for this project, in which strips of varying widths are stitched directly onto batting and backing fabric. Ribbon quilting is* *similar to the log-cabin technique but doesn't have a central block. Your Ribbon Jewelry Roll will make a splendid gift for a friend who loves to travel.*

SIZE: *7" × 15"*

MATERIALS

⅜ yard 45"-wide cotton print fabric

Scraps of six to eight cotton prints 10" in length

8" × 16" piece quilt batting

15" × 15" piece fusible interfacing

2½" strip ¾"-wide Velcro®

1¼ yards single-fold bias tape or 1"-wide bias strip

Sewing thread to match ⅜-yard fabric and bias tape

Trace and cut pattern for pocket flap from paper. From ⅜-yard fabric, cut two 7" × 15" rectangles and six flap pieces. From the fusible interfacing cut one 7" × 15" rectangle and three flap pieces. From scraps, cut 10" strips in widths varying from ¾" to 2".

Baste batting to wrong side of one rectangle. All seams are ¼". Place first fabric strip right side up diagonally across one corner of batting. Lining up raw edges, place second fabric strip right sides together with first strip. Stitch strips to batting and fabric. Fold second strip over so right side is facing up. Continue stitching strips to rectangle until entire piece is covered. See Diagram A. Trim excess batting and fabric strips.

To make inside pockets adhere interfacing rectangle to fabric rectangle with a hot iron. Press; then stitch one long edge of rectangle under ½" twice. Measure and mark three equal 5" pockets on rectangle. Lining up the raw edges, place pocket piece right side up on inside jewelry roll. Machine-stitch around outside edge of pocket rectangle and over marked lines, leaving top folded edge open. To make flaps, adhere interfacing to three flap pieces with a hot iron.

With right sides together stitch three interfaced flaps, leaving the top side open. Turn flaps right side out and press. Machine-topstitch over curved edge. Leaving ¼" seam allowance on both 7" sides of jewelry roll, and lining up top raw edges, baste flaps above pocket openings. See Diagram B.

See Binding Edges, page 20. Bind around outside edge of jewelry roll with bias tape. Cut three ½" and one 1" Velcro® strips. Stitch ½" Velcro® fastener under each flap. Folding the roll along the pocket edges; fold one side over the other. Stitch 1" Velcro® fastener to inside edge of jewelry roll. Stitch the opposite side of Velcro® fastener to outside center panel where Velcro® meets fabric.

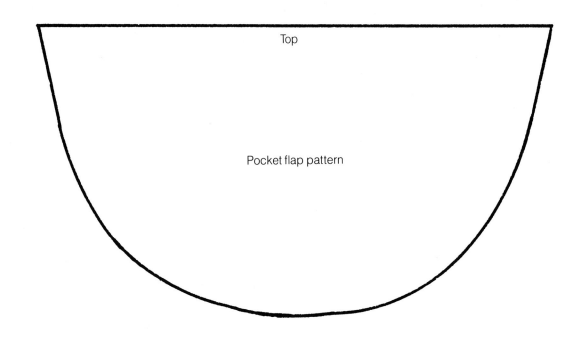

Top

Pocket flap pattern

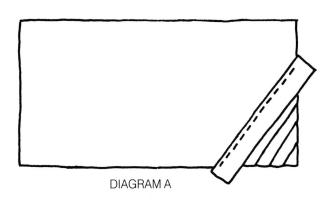

DIAGRAM A

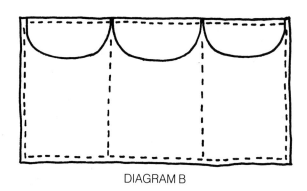

DIAGRAM B

◆ HEART-AND-LEAF SAFETY POUCH ◆

◆ *Both the design and the bold, primary colors used in this project were inspired by Pennsylvania Dutch folk art. The red heart and green leaves are appliquéd to both sides of the pouch. Red embroidery floss and contour quilting are then used around the appliqués.*

This "travel-smart" pouch will protect your alarm clock from the nicks and chips of a busy schedule. And it makes a splendid gift for a career-minded woman who is going places, the avid camper, or a student traveling away from home for the first time.

SIZE: 5″ × 5½″

MATERIALS *Cotton fabrics:*
- *4″ × 8″ piece white*
- *3″ × 6″ piece red*
- *3″ × 5″ piece green*
- *10½″ × 13″ piece blue*
- *10½″ × 13″ piece extra-loft quilt batting*
- *1 yard red single-fold bias tape*
- *1 yard red 6-strand embroidery floss*
- *Sewing thread to match fabrics*
- *White quilting thread*

Trace heart and leaf patterns. Cut from paper.

From red fabric cut two hearts, from green cut four leaves. From white fabric, cut two 4″ × 4″ squares. From blue fabric mark, then cut four 1¼″ × 4″ strips, four 1¼″ × 5½″ strips, two 1½″ × 6″ strips, and then one 6″ × 13″ rectangle.

With right sides together, stitch blue strips around outside edges of white squares with ¼″ seams. See Diagram A for stitching guide. Press all seams away from white fabric. Turning appliqué edges under ⅛″ as you sew, pin, then slip-stitch appliqués into place on white squares. With right sides together, machine-stitch squares together along bottom edge with ¼″ seam. Press seam open.

Mark quilting lines ¼″ outside of white squares. Sandwich quilt batting between appliquéd top piece and 6″ × 13″ piece of blue fabric. Baste layers together. With quilting thread, quilt ⅛″ inside appliqués and on marked quilting lines. Using two strands of 6-strand embroidery floss, contour-quilt around outside of appliqués ⅛″ from edges. Machine-zigzag along outside raw edge of top piece. Trim excess batting and fabric.

Press short sides of 1½″ × 6″ strips under ¼″ twice. Machine-stitch. Press long sides of strips under ¼″. Lining up the folded edges, press strips in half lengthwise. To make casing, center and place a folded strip along the top edge of each square; overlap square by ¼″. Machine-stitch along strip edge.

With right sides together and using ¼″ seams, stitch pouch sides below casing and bottom. Do not catch casing. Turn pouch right side out.

Press bias tape in half lengthwise and topstitch along edge. Cut tape into two equal pieces. Insert safety pin through end of one strip and push it through both sides of casing. Overlap ends and stitch together. Starting on opposite side of pouch, push remaining piece of tape through casing. Stitch ends together.

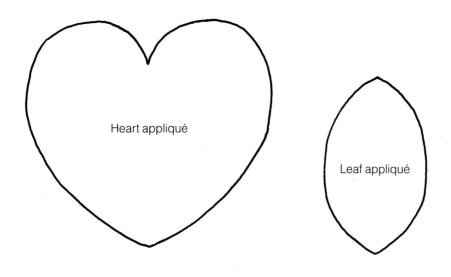

Heart appliqué

Leaf appliqué

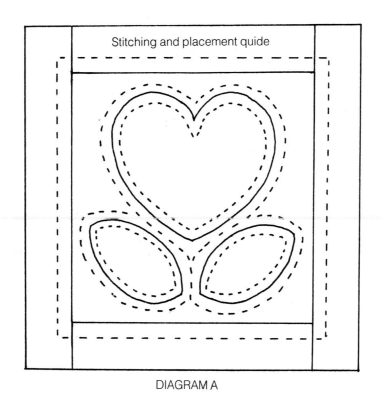

Stitching and placement guide

DIAGRAM A

◆ FIRST-AID BAG ◆

◆ *This bag is a perfect way to keep first-aid items handy…in a car's glove compartment…a gym locker…sailboat…or suitcase. Appliquéd and quilted, it's a soft-pack way to ensure that necessary first-aid remedies will always be on hand.*

SIZE: *7″ × 9″*

MATERIALS *Cotton fabrics:*
¼ yard 45″-wide white print
9″ × 14″ piece red print
Two 8″ × 11″ pieces extra-loft quilt batting
9″ white zipper
White quilting thread
Sewing thread to match fabrics

Trace cross patterns and cut from paper.

From red print fabric mark and cut one large cross, two small crosses, and two 1¼″ × 14″ bias strips. From white print, cut four 7½″ × 10″ rectangles.

Press one long side of each rectangle under ¼″. Following Diagram A, pin, then slip-stitch cross appliqués to one rectangle; turn appliqué edges under ¼″ as you sew. Place one side of zipper right side up under folded edge of appliquéd rectangle. Machine-topstitch ¼″ from zipper teeth. Stitch folded edge of another rectangle to unstitched zipper side.

To make bag lining, with wrong sides together, slip-stitch folded edges of remaining rectangles to underside of zipper ¼″ from zipper teeth. Mark vertical quilting lines 1″ apart on unappliquéd side of bag. Following stitching guide (broken lines) on Diagram B, mark quilting lines on appliquéd side of bag. Mark first quilting line ¼″ from outside edge of appliqués.

Making sure it is pushed against zipper edge, sandwich batting between lining and outside rectangles. Baste layers together.

Quilt over marked lines on unappliquéd side of bag. Quilt inside appliqués ¼″ from edges. Contour-quilt around outside of appliqués ⅛″ from edges and over marked lines. Stop quilt stitches ¼″ from bag edges. With closely spaced zigzag stitch, stitch along outside edge of bag. Trim excess batting, and then trim the corners slightly.

See Binding Edges, page 20. Stitch short side of bias strips together to make 26″ strip. With wrong sides together, bind around outside edge of bag with ¼″ seam; stitch bag together as you sew.

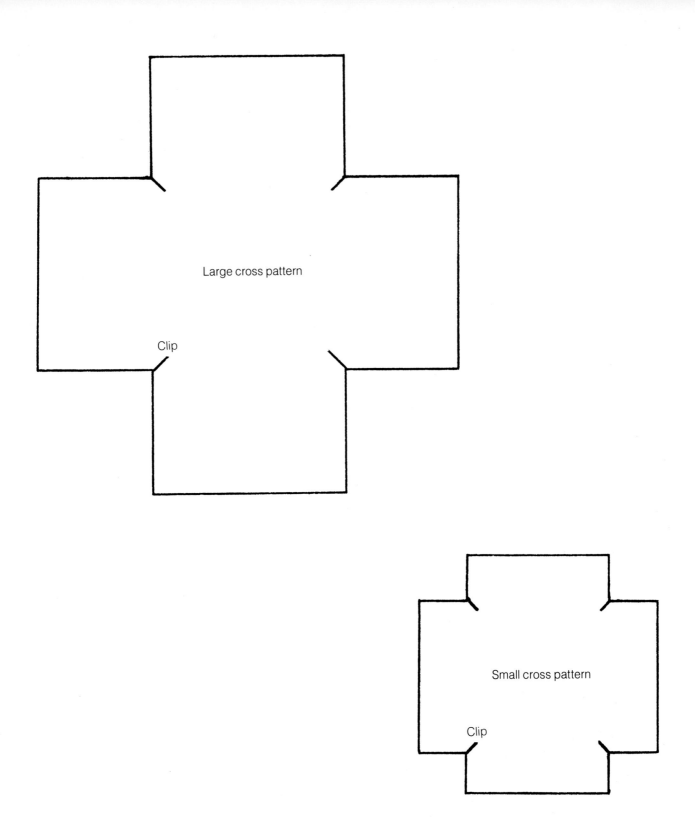

Large cross pattern

Clip

Small cross pattern

Clip

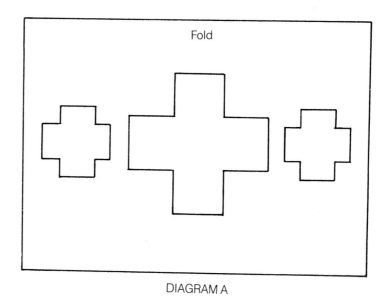

Fold

DIAGRAM A

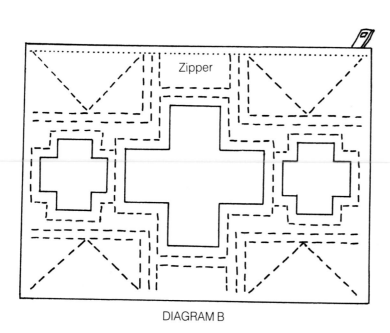

Zipper

DIAGRAM B

◆ TRAVELING SHOE BAG ◆

◆ *This sophisticated patchwork design is made by stitching large and small triangles together. Smart and functional, it's* *an ideal way to carry your shoes to work or fit them snugly in your luggage without soiling delicate fabrics.*

SIZE: 11½" × 13"

MATERIALS *Cotton fabrics:*
¾ yard 45"-wide solid green
¼ yard 45"-wide yellow with white polka dots
10" × 14" piece red print
Two 14" × 16" pieces extra-loft quilt batting
Red quilting thread
Sewing thread to match yellow and green fabrics

Trace pattern pieces. Cut from paper.

From green fabric mark and cut two 13" × 16" rectangles, four large triangles, four 3" × 12½" strips, and thirty-two small triangles. From polka-dot fabric mark and cut two 2" × 32" strips, sixteen small triangles, and two large triangles. From red print, cut sixteen small triangles and two large triangles.

All seams are ¼". Stitch a small green triangle to each print and polka-dot triangle along the diagonal to form thirty-two squares. Press seams open. To form center squares, following Diagram A, stitch one short side of each solid triangle to short side of each print and dot triangle to form four larger triangles. Stitch large triangles together along diagonal, forming two large squares. Press seams open.

Following Diagram B, stitch small squares into strips. Stitch strips along outside edge of each large square. Press seams open. With right sides together, stitch 3" × 12½" strip across bottom side of each patchwork square. Sandwich quilt batting between patchwork squares and 13" × 16" fabric squares. Baste layers together.

Following Diagram C (broken lines), machine-quilt ¼" in from seams. Machine-zigzag around outside edge of patchwork panels. Trim excess fabric and batting.

Press both short sides of remaining 3" × 12½" strips under ¼" twice and machine-hem. Press long sides of strips under ¼". Press strips in half lengthwise so folded edges meet.

To make bag casing, pin top of each panel ¼" inside each strip opening; leave ¼" panel seam allowance exposed at ends of strips. Machine-topstitch casing ⅛" from bottom edge. With right sides together, stitch bag sides and bottom; do not stitch through casing. Following Diagram D, box bottom corners by lining up side seam of bag with bottom seam and stitching ⅛" away from quilt stitches. Trim excess fabric. Turn bag right side out.

Press short sides of 2" × 32" strips under ¼". Press long sides under ¼". Press strips in half lengthwise so folded edges meet. Topstitch ⅛" from edge. Insert a safety pin through end of one strip and push it through both sides of bag casing. Stitch ends together. Starting on opposite side of bag, push remaining strip through casing. Stitch ends together.

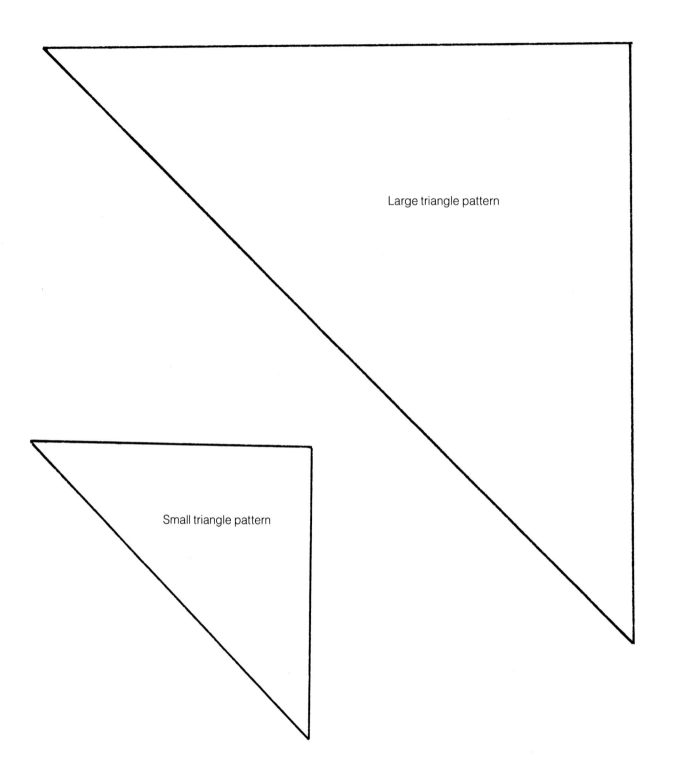

Large triangle pattern

Small triangle pattern

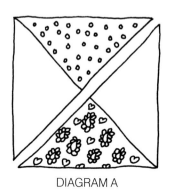

DIAGRAM A

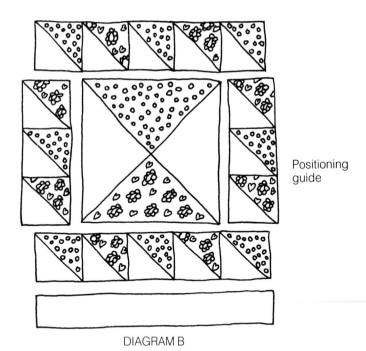

Positioning
guide

DIAGRAM B

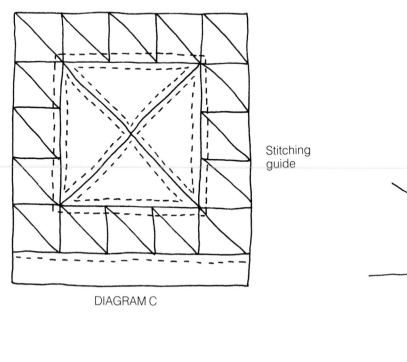

Stitching
guide

DIAGRAM C

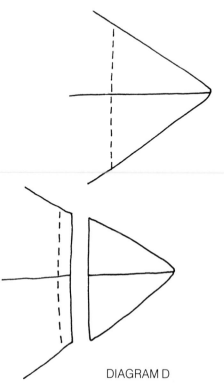

DIAGRAM D

BABY'S BEST

◆ BABY'S-BLOCK NAP PAD OR CARRIAGE COVER ◆

◆ *This is a sleepy-time nap pad that uses the traditional "baby's-block" pattern. It's stitched in pink, blue, and yellow fabrics—making it ideal for boy or girl.*

Baby's-Block Nap Pad makes a perfect baby-shower gift. And if you like, you can use fabrics printed with ducks, chicks, bunnies, or bears.

SIZE: 30" × 40"

MATERIALS *Cotton fabrics:*
- *1¾ yards 45"-wide light-blue print*
- *⅜ yard 45"-wide pink print*
- *¼ yard 45"-wide yellow print*
- *24" × 34" piece off-white*
- *33" × 43" piece quilt batting*
- *Sewing thread to match fabrics*
- *White quilting thread*

Trace pattern piece and cut from paper.

From blue, pink, and yellow fabrics cut six diamonds each. From blue fabric, cut two 4" × 34" strips and one 33" × 43" backing piece. From pink fabric, cut two 4" × 24" strips. From yellow fabric, cut four 4" × 4" squares and four 3½" × 3½" squares. Mark diagonal quilting lines 1" apart on white fabric.

All seams are ¼". With right sides together, stitch a blue, pink, and yellow diamond together to form a block. See Diagram A. Stitch six blocks. Press seam allowance away from lighter-colored fabric. Following Diagram B, stitch blocks together to make block appliqué. Trim excess seam allowance where points meet. Press raw edges under ¼". Center and pin block appliqué to white fabric. Slip-stitch into place.

To make top piece for nap pad, line up the raw edges and pin 3½" square to each corner of white fabric. Turn inside raw edges under ¼" and slip-stitch into place. With right sides together, stitch a blue strip to each long side of white fabric. Press seam allowance away from white fabric.

With right sides together, stitch 4" × 4" yellow square to both ends of each pink strip. Stitch a pink strip across top and bottom of pad top piece. Press seam allowance away from white fabric.

Centering the top piece on the batting sandwich, quilt batting between top piece and blue backing piece. Baste layers together.

Quilt block appliqué ¼" from all seams and ¼" from outside edge. Quilt over drawn quilting lines on white panel. Quilt squares and border strips ¼" from seam line, leaving outside edge unquilted.

Trim excess batting only. Self-bind outside edge of nap pad by turning edges of backing piece under ½" twice. Fold the bottom edges over the top piece and slip-stitch into place. Quilt ⅜" from outside edge of nap pad.

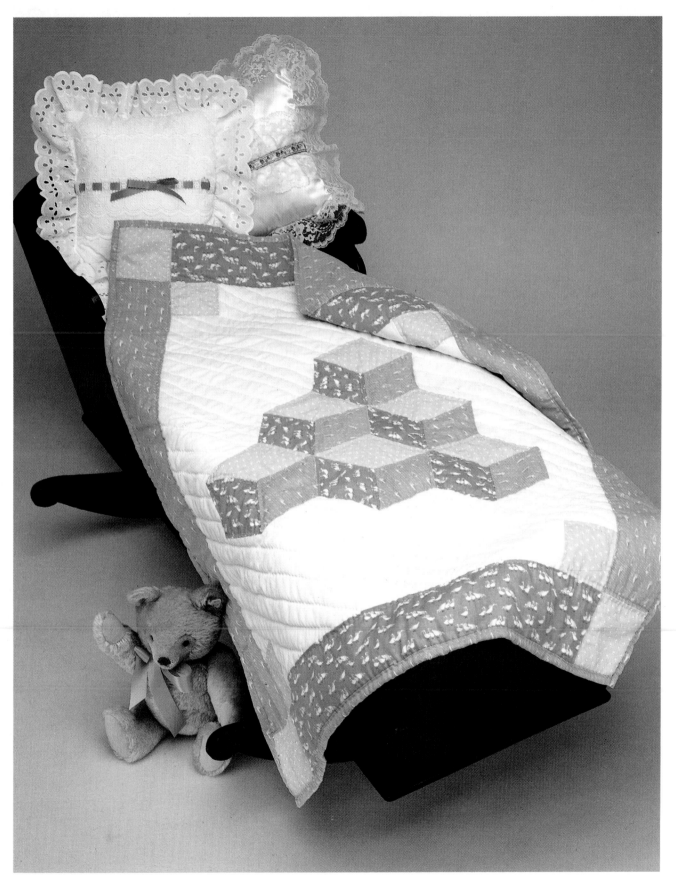

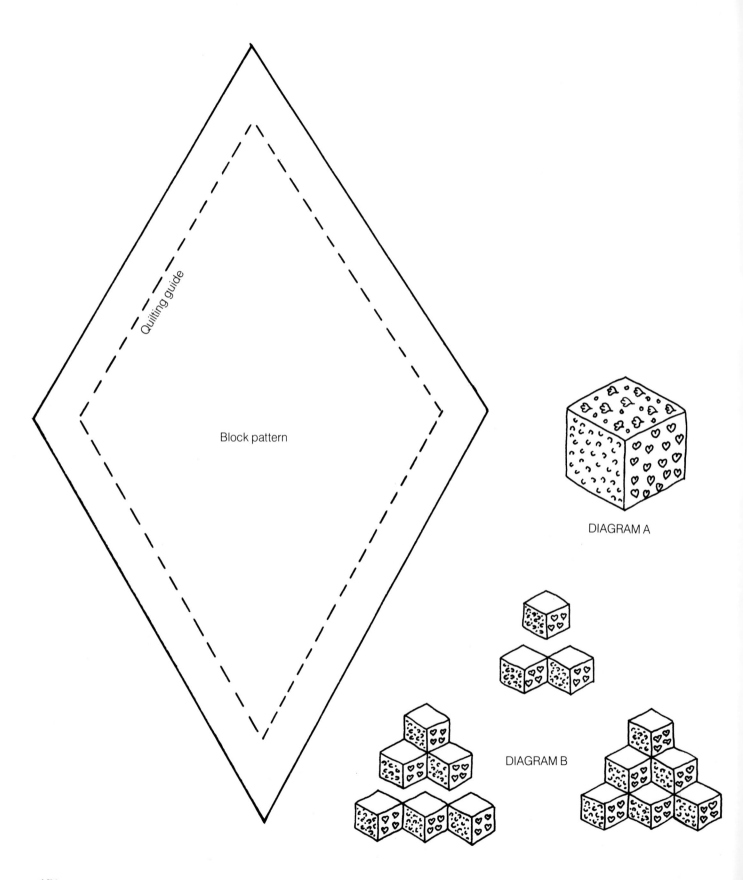

Quilting guide

Block pattern

DIAGRAM A

DIAGRAM B

◆ QUILTED CRITTERS ◆

◆ *Who wouldn't love these friendly patchwork friends? They're quilted and stuffed, and there's a heart appliquéd on* *each one. Make it from scraps...as a shower gift...bazaar best-seller...or as a cuddly toy for your favorite baby.*

SIZE: *8″ × 11″*

MATERIALS *Cotton fabrics:*

9″ × 12″ piece fabric for lamb back

9″ × 12″ piece muslin or any lightweight fabric

Scraps of solids, ginghams, and calicoes

2″ × 2½″ piece magenta

9″ × 12″ piece extra-loft quilt batting

6 oz. polyester stuffing

1 yard black 6-strand embroidery floss

½ yard ⅜″-wide satin ribbon

Quilting thread

Magenta and white sewing threads

CRITTER LAMB

See Enlarging Patterns, page 16. Enlarge pattern pieces. Cut from paper. Draw features on lamb face.

From solid scrap, cut two ears and one face piece. Draw features on face. Cut one heart from magenta fabric. From scraps, cut twenty-one 1¾″ × 1¾″ squares and ten 1″ × 9¼″ strips. Following Diagram A, arrange squares and strips in patchwork pattern. All seams are ¼″. Stitch squares together to form three strips of six squares each. Press seams open. Stitch 9¼″ strips together in rows of three each. Press seams open. With right sides together, stitch strips and squares together to form 9¼″ × 9¼″ patchwork square. Press seams open.

Trace lamb body onto right side of patchwork, lining up straight side of head with edge of fabric. See Diagram B. With right sides together, stitch lamb face to lamb body. Press seam open. With right sides together stitch ear pieces, leaving straight side open for turn-ing. Turn ear right side out and press. Following Diagram C, stitch ear to lamb head.

Following pattern diagram, pin, then machine-appliqué heart to lamb body with closely spaced zig-zag stitch. Sandwich quilt batting between patchwork and muslin. Baste layers together. Quilt lamb body in desired pattern. Quilt lamb face ½″ from outside edge. Machine-zigzag over outline of lamb body and along outside edge of face.

See Embroidery Stitches, page 22. Backstitch over mouth, drawing with black embroidery floss. Fill in eye and nose with satin stitch. Trim excess quilt batting and fabric. With right sides together, stitch lamb to 9″ × 12″ piece of fabric; leave 3″ opening along back leg for stuffing. Trim excess fabric, clip curves, and turn right side out.

Fill with polyester stuffing and slip-stitch opening closed. With satin ribbon, tie bow around lamb's neck.

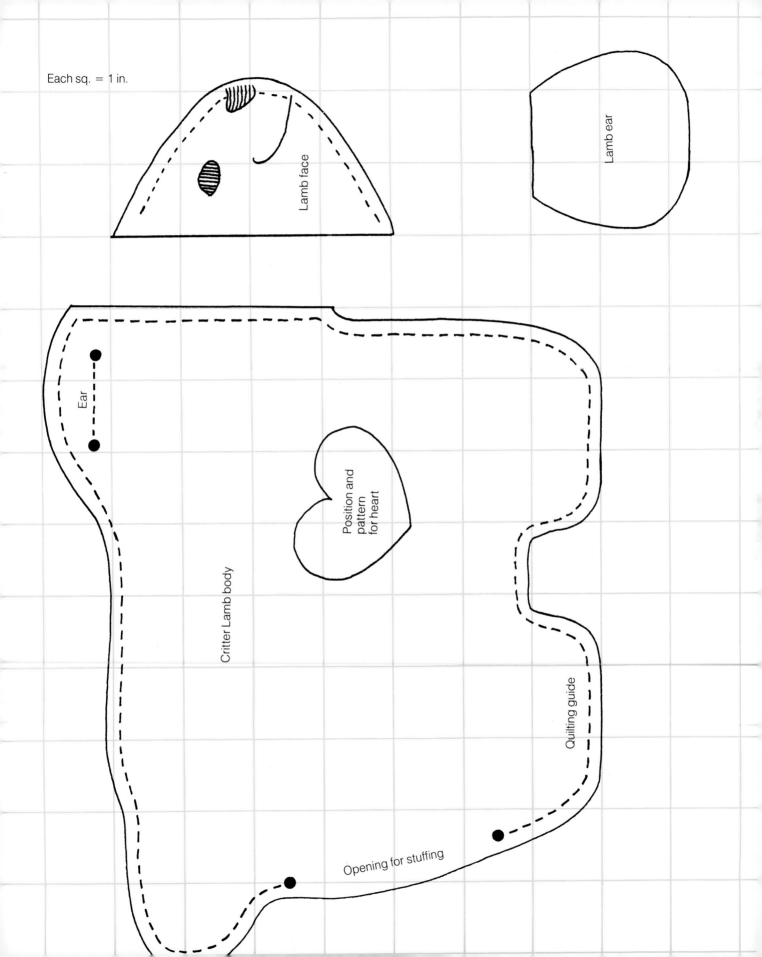

Each sq. = 1 in.

Lamb face

Lamb ear

Ear

Position and pattern for heart

Critter Lamb body

Quilting guide

Opening for stuffing

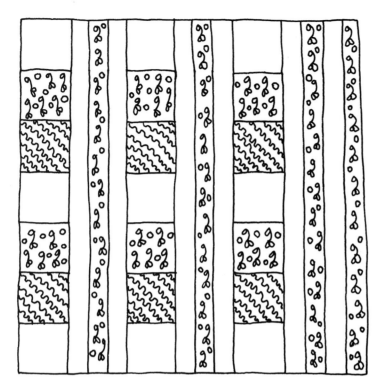

Lamb patchwork

DIAGRAM A

Lamb body position

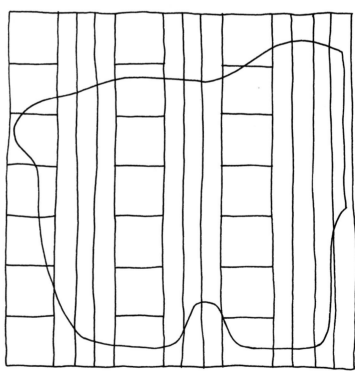

DIAGRAM B

Lamb ear position

DIAGRAM C

CRITTER BEAR

SIZE: 8″ × 10½″

MATERIALS *Cotton fabrics:*
  10″ × 13″ piece fabric for bear back
  10″ × 13″ piece muslin or any lightweight fabric
  Scraps of calicoes, ginghams, or solids
  2″ × 2½″ piece magenta
  3″ × 3½″ piece white
  10″ × 13″ piece extra-loft quilt batting
  6 oz. polyester stuffing
  1 yard black 6-strand embroidery floss
  ½ yard ⅜″-wide satin ribbon
  Quilting thread
  Magenta and white sewing threads

See Enlarging Patterns, page 16. Enlarge pattern pieces and cut from paper. Draw facial features on pattern of bear face.

Cut one heart from magenta fabric and one face piece from white fabric. Draw facial features on face. See Embroidery Stitches, page 22. Backstitch over mouth, drawing with black embroidery floss. Fill in nose and eyes with satin stitch.

From fabric scraps, cut twenty-four triangles. With ¼″ seam, machine-stitch triangles together along diagonal to form seventeen squares. Press seams open. Following Diagram A, arrange squares in patchwork pattern. Stitch squares together in strips with ¼″ seams. Press seams open. With right sides together and lining up seam lines, stitch strips together with ¼″ seams to form patchwork fabric. Press seams open.

Trace bear onto right side of patchwork. See Diagram B. Following pattern diagram, pin, then machine-appliqué heart and face to traced bear with closely spaced zigzag stitch. Sandwich quilt batting between patchwork and muslin. Baste layers together. Quilt inside each square ⅛″ from seams. Do not quilt outside traced outline.

Machine-zigzag over traced bear outline. Trim excess fabric and batting. With right sides together and using ¼″ seam, stitch patchwork bear to 10″ × 13″ piece of fabric. Leave 2½″ opening along one side for stuffing. Trim excess fabric, clip curves, and turn right side out. Stuff bear and slip-stitch opening closed. With satin ribbon, tie bow around bear's neck.

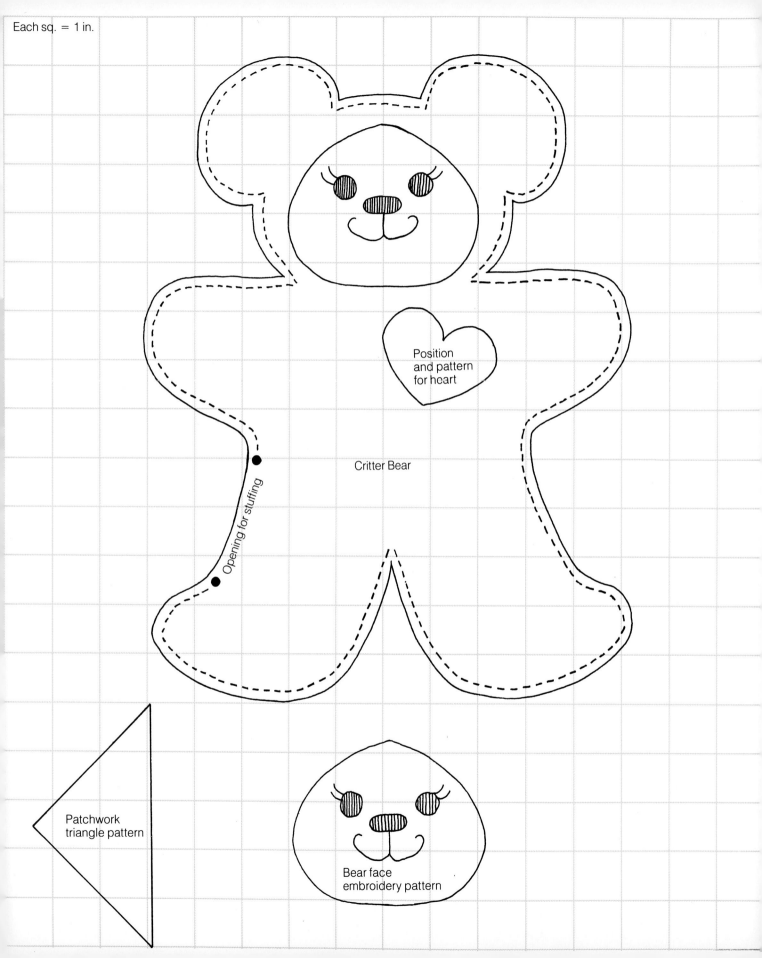

Each sq. = 1 in.

Position and pattern for heart

Critter Bear

Opening for stuffing

Patchwork triangle pattern

Bear face embroidery pattern

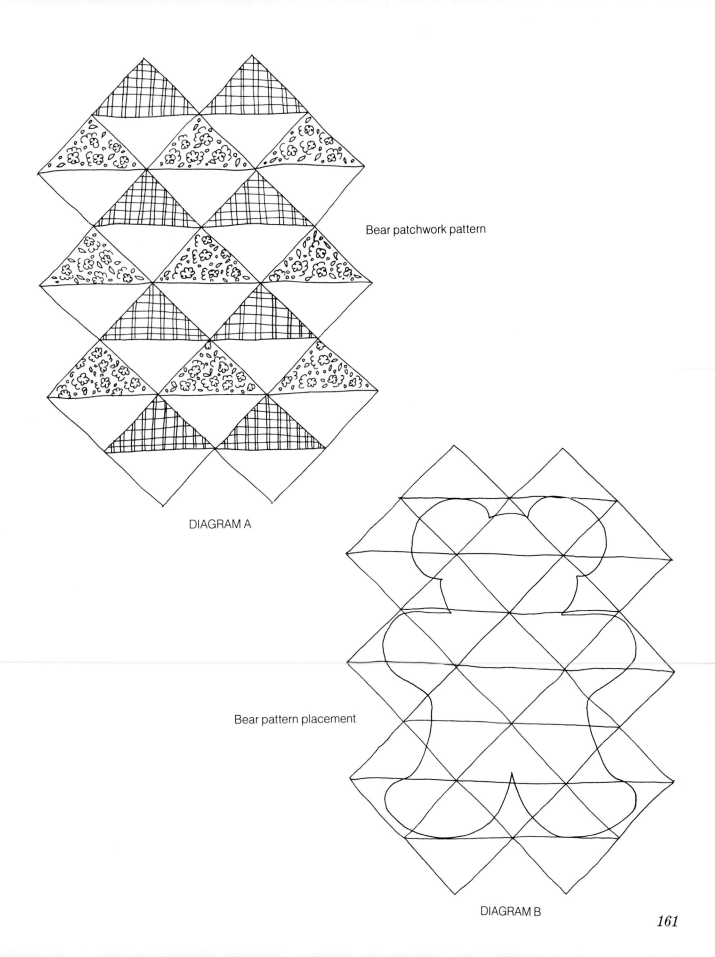

Bear patchwork pattern

DIAGRAM A

Bear pattern placement

DIAGRAM B

161

CRITTER BUNNY

SIZE: 7½" × 11"

MATERIALS *Cotton fabrics:*

11" × 13" piece fabric for bunny back

11" × 13" piece muslin or any lightweight fabric

Scraps of four to six different calicoes, stripes, or solids

2" × 2½" piece red

10" × 13" piece extra-loft quilt batting

6 oz. polyester stuffing

1 yard each black and dark-pink 6-strand embroidery floss

½ yard ⅜"-wide satin ribbon

Quilting thread

Red and white sewing threads

See Enlarging Patterns, page 16. Enlarge bunny and heart patterns. Cut from paper. Draw facial features on bunny pattern.

Cut one heart piece from red fabric. From fabric scraps, cut thirty 2½" × 2½" squares. Arrange squares in patchwork pattern, forming a rectangle of five by six squares. With ¼" seams, machine-stitch squares together in strips (five strips of six squares). Press seams open.

With right sides together, stitch strips with ¼" seams to form one 10½" × 12½" patchwork rectangle. Press seams open. See Diagram A. Trace bunny pattern onto right side of patchwork, drawing in facial features. Following pattern diagram, pin, then machine-appliqué heart to bunny's chest with a closely spaced zigzag stitch.

See Embroidery Stitches, page 22. Using pink embroidery floss, backstitch over mouth drawing. Fill in nose with pink satin stitch and eyes with black satin stitch. Draw diagonal quilting lines through centers of patchwork squares inside traced bunny. (See Diagram B, broken lines.) Sandwich quilt batting between patchwork and muslin. Baste layers together. Quilt over drawn lines.

Machine-zigzag over traced bunny outline. Trim excess fabric and batting. With right sides together and using ¼" seam, stitch patchwork bunny to 11" × 13" piece of fabric. Leave 3" opening along bottom of bunny for stuffing. Trim excess fabric, clip curves, and turn bunny right side out. Stuff bunny, then slip-stitch opening closed. With satin ribbon, tie bow around bunny's neck.

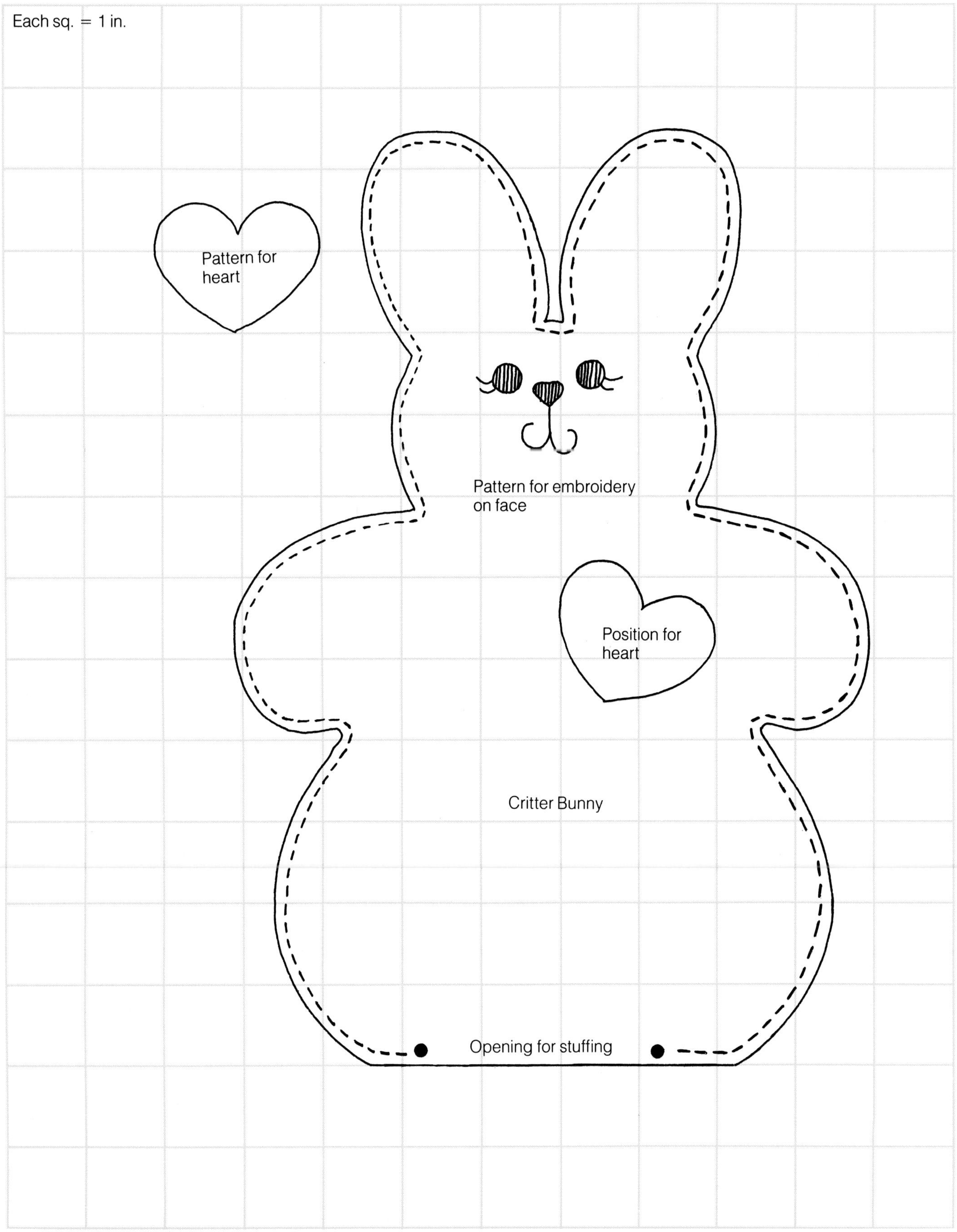

Each sq. = 1 in.

Pattern for heart

Pattern for embroidery on face

Position for heart

Critter Bunny

Opening for stuffing

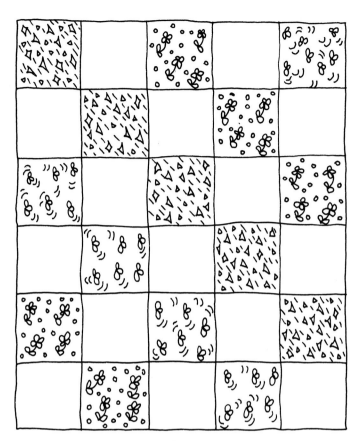

Bunny patchwork pattern

DIAGRAM A

Bunny pattern placement

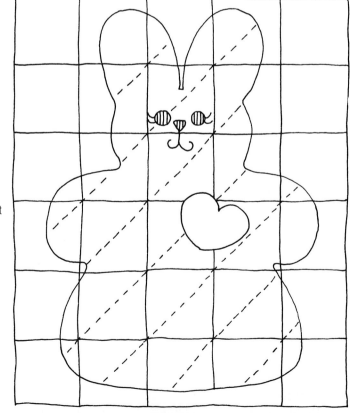

DIAGRAM B

INDEX

SMALL PATCHWORK AND QUILTING PROJECT IDEAS

◆ *For your home:*

Hot pads (for table)

Wall hangings

Stuffed wreaths

Valances (for curtains)

Throw for back of sofa or easy chair

Picture or mirror frame

Coffee table cloth (placed under glass)

Pillow shams

Entry bench pad

Picnic table quilt

Picnic basket liner with pocket for silverware

Plate warmer

◆ *For your personal use:*

Slippers

Vest

Album cover (for photos)

Notebook covers

Gym bag

Cassette tape bag

Apron appliqué

Quilted collar for sweater or blouse

Decorative padded shoulders

◆ *Baby projects*

Crib or carriage quilt

Baby blocks

Bunting

Bottle warmer

Booties

Tote bag

Stroller liner

For information on how you can have *Better Homes and Gardens* delivered to your door, write to: Mr. Robert Austin, P.O. Box 4536, Des Moines, IA 50336.